Critical Thinking:

Totality of Circumstances

(3rd ed.)

$$(\exists x)P(x) \neq (\forall x)P(x)$$

$$P \Rightarrow Q \neq Q \Rightarrow P$$

Wayne L. Davis, Ph.D.

Paul J. Leslie, Ed.D.

Jacquelyn L. Davis, B.S.

BALBOA.
PRESS

A DIVISION OF HAY HOUSE

Balboa Press books may be ordered through booksellers or by contacting:

Balboa Press
A Division of Hay House
1663 Liberty Drive
Bloomington, IN 47403
www.balboapress.com
1 (877) 407-4847

Because of the dynamic nature of the Internet, any web addresses or links contained in this book may have changed since publication and may no longer be valid. The views expressed in this work are solely those of the author and do not necessarily reflect the views of the publisher, and the publisher hereby disclaims any responsibility for them.

The author of this book does not dispense medical advice or prescribe the use of any technique as a form of treatment for physical, emotional, or medical problems without the advice of a physician, either directly or indirectly. The intent of the author is only to offer information of a general nature to help you in your quest for emotional and spiritual well-being. In the event you use any of the information in this book for yourself, which is your constitutional right, the author and the publisher assume no responsibility for your actions.

Any people depicted in stock imagery provided by Thinkstock are models, and such images are being used for illustrative purposes only.
Certain stock imagery © Thinkstock.

ISBN: 978-1-4525-9658-7 (sc)
ISBN: 978-1-4525-9659-4 (e)

Library of Congress Control Number: 2014907340

Printed in the United States of America.

Balboa Press rev. date: 05/06/2014

Preface

This book provides an overview of effectively understanding information. One goal of this book is for law enforcers to understand the legality of their actions via math, grammar, and logic. This book applies math and English to the law so that police officers may effectively articulate their actions in court. For example, specific laws and police actions can be evaluated via truth tables and Venn Diagrams. Some of the factors that can influence the value of information include assumptions, limitations, different lenses of truth, different ethical systems, different police department orientations, and the format in which the data are presented. For example, a suspect may attempt to mislead an officer by using existential and universal quantifiers and by using the converse of conditional statements. Another goal of this book is to apply basic math skills to common law enforcement scenarios. For example, the methods of determining angles, distances, and speeds are presented.

Authors

Wayne L. Davis, Ph.D.

Wayne L. Davis holds a Bachelor of Science in Electrical Engineering from the University of Michigan-Dearborn, a Master of Science in Business Administration from Madonna University in Livonia, Michigan, and a Ph.D. in Criminal Justice from Capella University in Minneapolis, Minnesota. In addition, Dr. Davis has earned a helicopter pilot license, an advanced open water scuba diver certification, a technician plus amateur radio license (N8ZFG), and a basic emergency medical technician certificate from the State of Michigan.

Dr. Davis has graduated from city, state, and federal law enforcement academies: Schoolcraft College in Livonia, Michigan, the Indiana Law Enforcement Law Academy, and the Federal Law Enforcement Training Center. He has over 20 years of law enforcement experience with city, state, and federal law enforcement agencies.

While he worked as a product design engineer at Ford Motor Company, Dr. Davis introduced the electronic engine control module into the pleasure boat industry. This included writing a product specification manual and performing test-to-failure statistical research. As a result, Dr. Davis was nominated for the Ford Motor Company Electronics Division Worldwide Leadership Excellence Award. Subsequently, this led to his research paper called, *A Study of Factors Affecting a Supply Decision by the Ford Motor Company International Division for Original Equipment*.

Dr. Davis has received the U.S. Customs & Border Protection Commissioner's Award, the U.S. Customs & Border Protection Scholastic Award, and he was appointed to a field-training officer by the Indiana State Police. In addition, Dr. Davis has conducted an exploratory research study called, *A Correlational Study of Childhood Religiosity, Childhood Sport Participation, and Sport-Learned Aggression among African American Female Athletes*. Subsequently, Dr. Davis has published several textbooks, which include a) *Report Writing for Police Officers*, b) *Police-Community Relations: Different Lenses & Perception of Truth*, c) *Interviewing, Interrogation, and Communication for Law Enforcement*, and d) *Terrorism, Homeland Security, and Risk Assessment through Research Proposal*.

Recently, Dr. Davis has created table top police scenes for which he has filed a patent. In addition, he has served as the Academic Coordinator for the Criminal Justice and Human Services Programs at Aiken Technical College in Aiken, SC. With the support of local law enforcement agencies, Dr. Davis has created an application-based criminal justice program that meets the needs of the local community.

Paul J. Leslie, Ed.D.

Paul J. Leslie holds a Bachelor of Arts in History from Armstrong Atlantic University in Savannah, Georgia and a Doctorate in Counseling Psychology from Argosy University in Sarasota, Florida.

Currently, he serves as Academic Coordinator of Psychology at Aiken Technical College where he is also an advisor in the Human Services degree program and teaches courses in abnormal psychopathology, substance abuse counseling and interviewing techniques.

Dr. Leslie is a Licensed Counselor and a Human Services - Board Certified Practitioner. He has a private practice in counseling, coaching and clinical hypnotherapy in Aiken, South Carolina. Dr. Leslie is the co-author of *Interviewing, Interrogation, and Communication for Law Enforcement* and *Get Out of Your Seat: An Average Passenger's Guide to Overcoming Airline Terror.*

Jacquelyn L. Davis, B.S.

Jacquelyn L. Davis holds a Bachelor of Science in Neuroscience from the University of Michigan. She has worked in the Health System Department of Neurology Laboratory at the University of Michigan, she has volunteered at the YWCA as a sexual assault advocate, and she has tutored students in the sciences at the Neutral Zone, which is a youth-driven teen center dedicated to personal growth through artistic expression, community leadership and the exchange of ideas. She currently works at Saint Mary's Hospital in Michigan as a patient care assistant in surgical services in the cancer department. It is her aspiration to become a physician.

Table of Contents

List of Tables

List of Figures

CHAPTER 1. CRITICAL THINKING

What is Critical Thinking?

The purpose of this book is to introduce or reintroduce the concept of critical thinking as it can be applied to the field of criminal justice. Our hope is that critical thinking is something that you begin to apply not only in your future work in the diverse areas of law enforcement, but also in most every other aspect of your own life.

To begin, we must define what specifically we mean by the term "critical thinking". This term can have multiple definitions pulled from a variety of sources. Throughout history, many teachers have believed that the effective utilization of thinking was something that needed to be taught to students so that they would be able to comprehend, learn, and, most importantly, apply the information they were given in the classroom to the environment outside of the academic setting.

According to Ruggiero (1995), "thinking is any mental activity that helps formulate or solve a problem, make a decision, or fulfill a desire to understand." Ruggiero further states that "thinking is an art, with its own purposes, standards, principles, rules, strategies, and precautions. And it is an art well worth learning for every important thing we do is affected by our habits of mind" (p.2).

Just because we are thinking, does that automatically mean that we are using "critical thinking"? When a person thinks something, does that mean what he or she thinks is automatically true and correct? Can we simply rely on what we think is true rather than investigate other viewpoints and still be successful in our professional and personal lives? As you will find out as you read through the chapters in this book, the answer to these questions is more than likely "no".

The ability to think critically is one of the most important activities we will perform in our lives. As we begin to think more critically about the world around us, we begin to become aware of the variety of beliefs and assumptions that many different people hold. We find that we start to notice how one's actions and beliefs may make sense in one situation but in other situations the same actions and beliefs appear nonsensical. We also notice that we are more open to alternate ideas that we may have previously dismissed without due consideration. By critically examining our thinking, we can become aware of our own biases and prejudices and begin to spot generalized, dogmatic, and dichotomous thinking that can occur in groups and organizations.

We also do not believe that critical thinking is something that should be regulated only to the field of academia but rather something that a person can use in most every area of his or her life. The more we approach the world from a perspective unbridled by rigid belief patterns set in stone, the more we can come closer to experiencing life as it is instead of seeing it through our own fixed "subjective reality tunnel vision".

According to Brookfield (1991), critical thinking is "reflecting on the assumptions underlying our and others' ideas and actions and contemplating alternative ways of thinking and living". When we use critical thinking, our decisions and beliefs are adopted only after carefully examining all available information instead of willfully adopting someone's model of the world without personal investigation. If a person decides to adopt critical thinking, he or she takes personal responsibility for his or her own beliefs and choices and, thus, becomes an active participant in determining how he or she lives his or her life. Paul and Elder (2002) state that "critical thinking is the disciplined art of ensuring that you use the best thinking you are capable of in any set of circumstances" (p.7). They further state that "if you are not progressively improving the quality of your life, you have not yet discovered the true power of critical thinking" (p.15).

Why use Critical Thinking?

We encourage the use of critical thinking because human beings tend to be misinformed, biased, prejudiced and unclear. As previously stated, the quality of our life is impacted by our ability to use critical thought. If a person does not examine his or her own thoughts, he or she will merely react to previously held beliefs that may or may not hold much truth. When a person reacts to the world through the viewpoint of unexamined thinking, he or she will often find that the previously mentioned biases and prejudices can get in the way of having a realistic view of any situation.

Psychologist Dr. Albert Ellis found in his research that people who do not examine and challenge their limiting and negative beliefs about themselves and the world around them tended to be more angry, depressed, and anxious in their daily lives. Ellis (2001) found that by merely challenging the negative thoughts that we possess, we can often change our emotions from disempowering feelings, which are based on faulty thinking about personal situations, to less harmful feelings, which are based on the reality of the situation.

An example of this would be a situation in which a man had a girlfriend who decided that she did not want to be romantically involved with him anymore. For most of us, it may be natural to feel sad and disappointed when a relationship does not work out the way one wants it to go. In this example however, the man is devastated because he thinks no one else will ever love him. His thoughts about this situation are a good example of someone not applying critical thinking to his own life.

For this man to hold this belief, he has to uncritically think the thought:

Girlfriend ending the relationship = No one will ever love me

If he were to critically examine his thoughts, he may find that his belief that no one else in the world will ever love him is based on some faulty premises.

Faulty Premise 1 - The man knows with absolute certainty what the rest of his life will be like even though he has not lived it.

Faulty Premise 2 - The man is absolutely certain that in a world consisting of billions of people, most of whom he does not know, there is not at least one person who may love him.

His unchallenged thoughts and beliefs about his relationship are what have caused him excessive emotional discomfort; his discomfort is not simply the consequence of the ended relationship. When examining this example critically, we can see that the only "reality" in the scenario was that the girlfriend decided to leave the relationship. Everything else was a product of the man's unexamined negative thoughts. By being open to critically examining what he thinks and whether or not it has validity, the man can move from disempowered thinking and feelings to a more realistic view of the situation.

Paul and Elder (2009) assert that if a person adopts critical thinking, the person will be more likely to accurately raise important questions when faced with a problem. The person will be able to better gather and interpret relevant information pertaining to the problem, will be able to think in a more open-minded manner by examining alternative ideas and beliefs about the problem, and will be able to reach a carefully formed solution or outcome about the problem, which can be effectively communicated to others. Paul and Elder write "critical thinking is, in short, self-directed, self-disciplined, self-monitored and self-correcting thinking" (p.2).

Components of Thought in Critical Thinking

In order to use more critical thinking in our lives, it is important to understand the components of thought that create the structure of thinking. Elder and Paul (2005) created a model that assigns thought into eight different elements that are used when employing critical thinking:

1. **Generates a Purpose – goals or objectives**
2. **Raises Questions - the particular issue at hand**
3. **Uses Information – using data, facts, observations, experiences**
4. **Makes Interpretations and Inferences – conclusions, solutions**
5. **Utilizes Concepts – use of theories, definitions, principles, models**
6. **Makes Assumptions – axioms, presuppositions**
7. **Generates Implications – consequences**
8. **Embodies a Point of View – frame of reference, perspectives**

Here is an example of how this could be applied to a situation in which someone is entering into a specific work related project or task. If he or she is using the art of critical thinking, he or she could ask the following questions of himself or herself as he or she moves through the various stages of completing the project.

1. **Generates a Purpose** – What is my outcome? What am I specifically attempting to achieve with this project? Is my purpose of doing this project self-serving or does it take into consideration other people?

2. **Raises Questions** – Am I able to specifically state my questions about the project in a precise manner? Are the questions I am raising pertinent to the project?

3. **Uses Information** – Are my assertions about the project supported by evidence? Is the information I have gathered relevant to the ideas I am putting forth? What other questions do I need to ask that have not been previously asked?

4. **Makes Interpretations and Inferences** – Have I clearly articulated the conclusions I put forth for the project? Are my conclusions reasonable and do they have merit? Do my conclusions of the information contradict the evidence given?

5. **Utilizes Concepts** – What is the main concept I am using in working on this project? Am I using the concept in an appropriate manner?

6. **Makes Assumptions** – Are my assumptions about this project clearly based on credible information? Do any of my assumptions contradict other assumptions that I have based this project on?

7. **Generates Implications** – Have I considered the consequences for making this particular decision for the project? If I make this decision, what other consequences could happen for which I have not accounted?

8. **Embodies a Point of View** – Have I considered other points of view regarding this project? Am I emotionally invested in only seeing one point of view about this project?

According to Elder and Paul (2005), each of these structures can have implications upon the other structures. For example, changing the purpose of what one is critically examining may have consequences on the questions that develop. To ensure quality thinking, it is important to apply Universal Intellectual Standards to our thinking process. When a person learns these standards and incorporates them into his or her way of thinking, the person often notices how much more precise and understandable his or her thinking can become and how much more insight one has into the particular issue at hand (Elder and Paul, 2005).

Universal Intellectual Standards

1. **Clarity** – "Could you give me more information about that?" "Can you give an example?" If a statement is not clear, a person will not be able to determine if the statement is realistic or accurate. For example, suppose a speaker asks, "What can be done about the issue of homelessness in the United States?" This is a very unclear question. In order to directly address the question, the listener would have to

have a clear comprehension of what the speaker considers to be the "issue". A question with much more clarity would be, "What specific actions can the government of the United States take to assist people who are destitute?" Due to the increased clarity, a respondent now has a better guide to think about the topic.

2. **Accuracy** – "How could this be verified in an objective manner?" "How can this be determined to be true?" Just because a statement is clear does not automatically make the statement valid. For example, "Most people prefer chocolate ice cream to vanilla ice cream". In order to be credible, this sentence would need to give some evidence that supports the assertion. One could ask, "How many people were asked this question?" "Who were in the sample group that was asked about the ice cream flavor?" "What groups were not asked about the flavors?"

3. **Precision** – "Could you be more specific about that?" "Could you give more details concerning that?" Even though a statement can be both clear and accurate, it may not be precise. For example, suppose a speaker states, "Mary is unhealthy". In this example, we do not know the speaker's definition of the term "unhealthy". In order to enhance the precision of our communication, we need to transmit enough details so that the receiving party can comprehend what is meant. A better statement may be, "Mary has respiratory problems due to her habit of smoking two packs of cigarettes a day, performing no exercise, and eating nothing but fatty foods."

4. **Relevance** – "How does this relate to the question?" "How does this help understand the issue?" Although statements may have clarity, accuracy, and precision, the statements may not necessarily be relevant to the issue. For example from our previous example, just because Mary is deemed "unhealthy" does not necessarily have a bearing on whether she is an effective employee. If something is relevant to an issue, then it is directly connected with, and may have an effect on, that particular issue.

5. **Depth** – "What are some of the difficulties dealing with this issue?" "What makes this problem complex?" If our thinking is deep enough, we can identify underlying issues and complexities involved in a particular problem. If a statement is lacking in depth, it often will not address the underlying elements that have created certain conditions. For example, suppose someone states, "The reason teenagers try alcohol is because it is illegal to do so." There is little depth to this statement. This statement does not take into account elements such as peer pressure, the desire to be accepted by peers, unhappy home lives, the modeling of parents who drink, etc. The statement has not considered the many extraneous variables that may have an impact on teenage alcohol consumption.

6. **Breadth** – "From what other perspectives do I need to examine this issue?" "What other points of view would be beneficial?" If we consider an issue from every viewpoint that is relevant, then we think in a broad way. If we fail to give any attention to other possible perspectives, then our thinking is incomplete and limited. For many of us, some points of view that strongly disagree with our own beliefs can feel threatening. If we choose to ignore perspectives simply because they cause personal discomfort, then we bind our thinking to a one-dimensional perspective.

7. **Logic** – "Does the statement agree with the evidence given?" "Does this make sense when all the information is considered together?" When we examine information, we bring together a various array of thoughts. When these thoughts make sense in combination and support the evidence given, then the thinking could be considered logical. If, however, the combined thoughts do not support each other or the evidence, then the thoughts are illogical. For example, Tony has been repeatedly informed that reading the chapters in the book and taking notes in class will improve his grade. Tony observes other students following those same instructions and earning good grades. However, Tony concludes that taking notes in class and reading the chapters in the book will not help him because he has always done poorly in school. Tony is clearly making an illogical decision.

8. **Significance** – "Which of the facts connected to this problem are the most important?" "Do I understand the central concept?" When we think about an issue, we need to take into account the most important aspects of the issue. It is important to recognize that not all of the information given is of equal importance. As a result, many times we fail to ask the most important questions and we focus on superficial issues. Focusing on topics of little importance is a waste of effort and resources. In college, for example, instead of attempting to learn the material, students often ask, "Is this going to be on the test?" "What do I need to do to get an "A" in this course?" Focusing only on these types of questions may limit the overall performance in class and the fundamental understanding of the subject being studied.

9. **Fairness** – "Am I biased toward one point of view and, if so, has it affected my judgment?" In order to think critically, we want to ensure that our thinking is in context and congruent with reason. Individuals often participate in thinking that can be described as self-deceptive. We will sometimes only consider things that support our own beliefs and ideas. When we reach a conclusion about an issue, we want to ensure that the assumptions we are using to arrive at that particular conclusion are fair and congruent with the facts related to the issue. For example, consider the statement, "People from the North are rude and quick tempered." This statement is based on prejudice and stereotypes, which are based on faulty assumptions. The truth is that there are many people who act rude and have quick tempers in the North and there are also many people who are polite and are calm in the North. When we use sweeping generalizations that are not justified and are based on faulty assumptions, we may make large and damaging errors.

In summary, critical thinking can be identified in the contexts of our professional actions, social interactions, and interpersonal relationships. As stated in Brookfield (1991), critical thinking "involves calling into question the assumptions underlying our customary, habitual ways of thinking and acting and then being ready to think and act differently on the basis of this critical questioning" (p.1).

As you move through the next chapters, you will be given information and a variety of exercises that are designed to specifically enhance your ability to think critically in the area of criminal justice. Our hope is that by learning critical thinking in this particular area, these concepts for thinking will eventually cross over to the other areas of your life. We believe this to be a good thing because people who consistently employ critical thinking hold a high degree of integrity via continual pragmatic and honest self-examination. A person will become more rational and solution-oriented the more a person practices critical thinking. All of this can lead to a life free from dogmatic, limiting beliefs, which can hamper our sense of fulfillment and happiness.

Applying Critical Thinking Skills

Critical thinking is the open-minded, dynamic, and reflective process of collecting, analyzing, evaluating, and applying information in order to make best-practice decisions (Aiken Technical College, 2013). In law enforcement, police officers employ critical thinking skills when they evaluate the totality of the circumstances in order to establish probable cause and make decisions. In other words, police officers make the best decisions possible based on the available information. If the available information changes, then police officers should reassess the data and, perhaps, change their position; failure to change their position when the new data indicate that the initial decision was wrong is bad police work. Furthermore, police officers must understand that all decisions rely on assumptions. This is true because humans have limited intelligence. Indeed, if humans knew everything in the universe, then there would never be the need for a trial.

Suppose that the driver of a vehicle admitted that he had been drinking alcoholic beverages. In addition, he had bloodshot eyes, he had slurred speech, he exhibited poor driving behaviors, and he failed the field sobriety tests. The defense attorney may attack the problem by attempting to dismiss the totality of circumstances. The defense attorney may ask the police officer in court whether a person who admits that he had been drinking is necessarily intoxicated. The police officer's answer will be "no." The defense attorney may then ask the police officer if a person is intoxicated because he has bloodshot eyes. The police officer's answer will be "no." The defense attorney might then ask the police officer if a person is intoxicated because he has slurred speech. The police officer's answer will be "no." The defense attorney may then ask the police officer if a person is intoxicated because he was speeding. The police officer's answer will be "no." The defense attorney might then ask the police officer if a person is intoxicated because he failed the one leg stand test. The police officer's answer will be "no." In the end, the defense attorney will have shown that the police officer admitted that every test that the driver failed does not indicate that the driver was intoxicated. The defense attorney is attempting to get the jury to assess each factor independently. In short, each factor in and of itself is not enough to show guilt beyond a reasonable doubt.

However, the prosecutor may address the situation by considering the totality of circumstances (i.e., linking all of the factors together). For example, if each variable is cumulative, then being involved in a crash, admitting drinking, having bloodshot eyes, having slurred speech, failing field sobriety tests, and other incriminating evidence may all add up to a 95% confidence level of guilt. This may be enough to find the suspect guilty beyond a reasonable doubt. Thus, each factor considered will move the suspect inward from one concentric ring to the next concentric ring. Once the suspect hits the center of the target, that suspect is intoxicated. The jury might be more likely to convict a suspect if the prosecutor can distinguish the suspect from the jurors. In other words, the jurors do not want to be arrested for having bloodshot eyes. Thus, they may not convict a suspect unless the prosecutor can show that the suspect is different from them in a meaningful way. This is exactly what the prosecutor attempts to do as he or she continually moves inward from one concentric ring to the next until the center of the target is reached. See *Figure 1*.

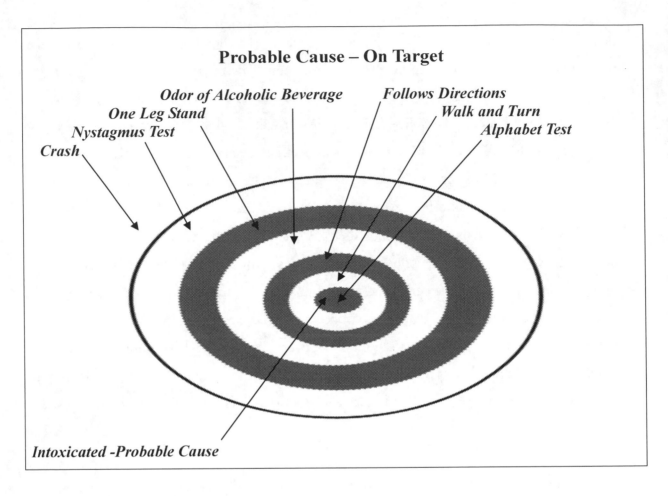

Figure 1. Totality of Circumstances.

Objective: Understanding Data

- Better decisions can be made if data are better understood

- Individuals who more educated about a topic can more effectively utilize available resources

- Discussing trends without understanding the data can contribute toward the problem

- Educated individuals need to challenge the validity of the data

Exercise 1: Watch you assumptions!

Use the information below to make your decision.

City	2012 Reported Crime	2013 Reported Crime
A	100,000	100,000
B	100,000	200,000

After the 2013 results are published, you plan to move to either City A or City B. Which city is safer? Use critical thinking to explain the reasoning for your answer.

See the end of this chapter for the answer to Exercise 1.

Crime

- Not all crime may be bad behavior (e.g., Galileo)

- Some illegal activities are demanded (e.g., drugs)

- Deviance is described as the source of innovation that attacks traditional thinking at the core level (Perkins, 2002).

Who Defines Deviant Behavior?

Different interest groups struggle for power and the group that comes out on top establishes what is considered normal behavior. The behaviors considered abnormal or "deviant" are defined by the dominant interest group, which then creates laws to punish such behaviors.

 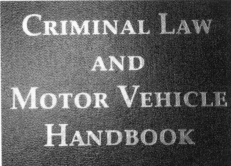

Who Maintains Order?

- There are about 400 U.S. residents for every full-time sworn police officer (Reaves, 2007; U.S. Department of Labor, 2009)

- Law and order depend upon residents submitting themselves to the government in order to be governed; law enforcement requires that people voluntarily comply with the law and assist with law enforcement efforts (Carter, 2002)

- Most law enforcement is done by community members and not by the police (Carter, 2002)

- Community members are the ones who set the standards for socially acceptable behaviors (Schmalleger, 2011)

- Because people voluntarily submit to the government's authority, it is the government's job to serve its people (Cain, 2003).

Critically Examining "Deviance"

Example: <u>Marijuana Law</u> (Gahlinger, 2004; Yaroschuk, 2000)

- William Hearst was a wealthy newspaper publisher (1880s)

- Hearst owned millions of acres of trees (wood)

- Hearst did not like the hemp plant because it made better paper compared to wood

- To minimize the profit loss due to hemp, Hearst linked marijuana to the crime rate in New Orleans. The purpose was to sell more newspapers (customers demand exciting stories) and to outlaw marijuana (hemp) for future business.

- During the Great Depression (which started in 1929), the horrific lack of employment in the United States led to a negative view of Mexicans, who were also seeking jobs. They were viewed as "unwelcomed labor".

- Hearst used the media to create a stereotype that all Mexicans used marijuana and that they were dangerous and frenzied. Texas, California, Arizona, and Colorado joined Hearst's media assault to force Mexicans out of the U.S.

- Hearst's Goal: use the media against the Mexican population and to gain state support to outlaw marijuana so that hemp does not replace wood as the major supplier of paper.

- Hearst's Tactic: exaggerate the effects of marijuana to feed the fear of the general population toward Mexicans and hemp.

- The Result: Marihuana Tax Act 1937, which stated that a person needed a specific stamp to purchase Marijuana. However, all stamp applications were denied. Currently, marijuana is illegal in most areas of the United States.

- In essence, the original push for making marijuana illegal was for financial gain. Minorities were targeted and discriminated against to achieve this financial goal.

Crime Control – Police Officers

- Officers cannot enforce the law if they do not know the law

- Officers must understand the viewpoints of the community members being served

- Officers must communicate their own viewpoints effectively

Summary

- Investigators need to evaluate the source of the data

- Investigators need to know the limitations and assumptions of the data

- Law enforcers need to align the assumptions of a crime preventative technique with assumptions of the theory used to explain the causes of that particular crime. For example, it is a waste of resources to attempt to deter crime via the deterrence theory, which requires rational thought, if the cause of the crime is due to biochemical problems within the brain, which is preventing rational thought.

When attempting to accomplish a goal, officers need to set **SMART** objectives (Walker, 2012). Objectives are benchmarks used as reference points to assess performance as the officer works toward an overall goal. Objectives should be **S**pecific, **M**eaningful, **A**ttainable, **R**elevant, and **T**imely.

Answer to Exercise 1

Insufficient data to answer question.

1) City A is currently safer if everything else is equal and if the crime rate in City B has doubled.

2) City B is currently safer if City B hired more police officers, who have arrested more of the criminals. The streets are now safer.

3) City A = City B if the arrest rate was manipulated by one simple command. For example, the police chief in City B may have ordered officers to file two charges for each event in order to double the arrest rate (perhaps to show that the crime rate is high in order to receive funds). For example, for each DUI investigation, police officers may be told to file DUI per se and DUI faculties impaired (i.e., two arrests for one event). After funds are received, the police chief may revoke his order in order to prove that greater funds mean fewer crimes. By doing this, the police chief is able to control the crime rate at will.

References

Aiken Technical College (2013). Retrieved from http://www.atc.edu/p371.aspx

Brookfield, S.D. (1991). *Developing critical thinkers: Challenging adults to explore alternative ways of thinking and acting.* San Francisco, CA: Jossey-Bass

Cain, W. (2003). Declaring independence. *Society, 41* (1).

Carter, D. (2002). *Issues in police-community relations: Taken from The Police and the community* (7th ed.). Boston, MA: Pearson.

Elder, L. and R. Paul (2005). *The guide to critical thinking: Concepts and tools.* Dillon Beach, CA: Foundation for Critical Thinking.

Ellis, A. (2001). *Overcoming destructive beliefs, feelings, and behaviors.* Amherst, NY: Prometheus Books.

Gahlinger, P. (2004). *Illegal drugs: A complete guide to their history, chemistry, use, and abuse.* New York, NY: Plume.

Paul, R. and Elder, L. (2009). *The foundation of analytic thinking: How to take thinking apart and what to look for when you do.* Dillon Beach, CA: Foundation for Critical Thinking.

Paul, R.W. and Elder, L. (2002). *Critical thinking: Tools for taking charge of your professional and personal life.* Upper Saddle River, NJ: Pearson.

Perkins, C. (2002). In support of deviance. *ID, 38*(4).

Reaves, B.A. (2007). Census of state and local law enforcement agencies, 2004. *Bureau of Justice Statistics Bulletin.* Retrieved from http://bjs.ojp. usdoj.gov/index.cfm?ty =dcdetail&iid=249

Ruggiero, V.R. (1995). *The art of thinking: A guide to critical and creative thought (*4th Ed. New York, NY: Harper Collins.

Schmalleger, F. (2011). *Criminology: A brief introduction.* Boston, MA: Prentice Hall

U.S. Department of Labor, Bureau of Labor Statistics (2009). *Occupational outlook handbook, 2010-11 edition.* Retrieved from http://www.bls.gov//oco/ocos/60.htm

Walker, D.C. (2012*). Mass notification and crisis communications: Planning, preparedness, and systems.* Boca Raton, FL: CRC.

Yaroschuk, T. (Producer & Writer). (2000). *Hooked: Illegal drugs and how they got that way* (Vol. 1) [Motion Picture]. The History Channel: A&E.

CHAPTER 2. PERSPECTIVES OF TRUTH & PURPOSE

What is Truth?

Before police officers can effectively serve the public, they must first understand the public. However, groups of individuals may experience life's events differently from other groups, and one community member may perceive reality differently from another community member. Although not all-inclusive, the following discussion describes several different perspectives of truth. A police officer who understands that there are different interpretations of reality will be able to better serve a greater population. Indeed, a single event may be considered acceptable in one culture yet taboo in another. In short, there are different perceptions of truth based on different references in which to interpret data. If an officer believes that his or her truth is the only truth, then that officer will be at a disadvantage when dealing with other people.

Positivists argue that the world is ordered and that reality is something to be captured, studied, and understood (Hatch, 2002). Positivists rely on facts, laws, and theories to make predictions. This can be accomplished via experiments, studies, and surveys. Positivists believe that the researcher is an objective and neutral data analyst.

Logical positivists argue that an objective reality exists and is independent of human mind and human behavior (Crossan, 2003). Logical positivists believe that the human experience of the world reflects an objective, independent reality (Weber, 2004). It is this reality that is used as the foundation for human knowledge in the building of a reality beyond the human mind. Logic positivism argues that people are objects whose behaviors can be reliably predicted (Crossan).

Post positivists argue that reality exists but cannot be fully understood or realized due to limited human intelligence (Hatch, 2002). Post positivists believe that knowledge is produced through generalizations and approximations via rigorously defined qualitative studies and low level statistics. To post positivists, the researcher is the data collection instrument.

Post modernists argue that knowledge is partial, fragmented, and contingent (McLaughlin & Muncie, 2006). Indeed, reality and science are socially constructed (Holliday, 2007). In other words, everything in life that is perceived is conditioned by culture, interactions, and institutions. Life's events occur by chance and, although humans are role-makers, their roles are unstable constructions (McLaughlin & Muncie). To post modernists, discourses are a linguistic coordinate system, and language is very influential.

Constructivists reject scientific realism and argue that there are multiple subjective realities and that absolute realities are unknowable (Glesne, 2006; Hatch, 2002). Constructivists believe that knowledge is symbolically constructed and that various realities are constructed via individual perspectives. To constructivists, investigators and participants determine truth through mutual agreement.

Post structuralists argue that there is no truth and that order is created within an individual's mind in order to give meaning to the universe (Hatch, 2002). Post structuralists believe that events happen for no particular reason and that there are multiple realities, each being equally valued. Truth is subjective, local, and constantly changes.

Pragmatists believe that truth is defined by what is effective, useful, and brings about positive consequences (Mertens, 2005). Pragmatists avoid the metaphysical concepts of truth and reality because they involve useless debates and discussions. To pragmatists, truth is measured in terms of accomplishment and resolution.

Critical theorists and **feminists** argue that the world consists of historically situated structures that have a real impact on the lives of individuals based on race, social class, and gender and that knowledge is subjective and political (Hatch, 2002). Critical theorists focus on race and social class while feminists focus on gender. Critical theorists and feminists believe that there is a differential treatment of individuals based on race, social class, and gender and that these factors limit opportunities for certain groups of people. Specifically, the poor, minorities, and females are discriminated against in society and are generally at a disadvantage.

Feminist criminology is "a developing intellectual approach that emphasizes gender in criminology" (Schmalleger, 2007, p. G-11). According to feminists, men have dominated the field of criminal justice and have developed theories and written laws for the explanation and control of crime based on their own perspectives (Akers & Sellers, 2009). Indeed, traditional criminal justice theories make no distinction between men and women (Schmalleger). Although some theories may be applied to both men and women, such as the social bonding theory and the biological theory, the traditional criminology theory inadequately accounts for crimes committed by females (Akers & Sellers). Currently there is no single well-developed theory that explains female crime.

In order to better understand female criminality and to address the root causes of female crime, females need to be incorporated into the development of criminal theories (Schmalleger, 2007). After all, women make up about half of the U.S. population and first-hand information is optimal (i.e., their perspective is essential). Because women obtain unique understandings of reality based on their social and personal positions within society, their perceptions of crime may be different from men's perspective of crime (Hammers & Brown, 2004). Thus, because the criminal justice system is predominately run by men, who use their own realities to make social policies, these policies may be ineffective involving half of the U.S. population (i.e., women) because they may be based on flawed assumptions (i.e., they assume that there is no behavioral difference between men and women). Indeed, women's perception of truth, which is created by their personal experiences involving social class, culture, and race, may not be adequately represented in the current criminal justice system (Weber, 2004).

For females to effectively influence public policies, they must be equally represented within state and federal government positions. Although this may be opposed by people in power, laws need to be passed that demand 50% of all state and federal public offices be held by females. In this way, the female population would be adequately represented in positions that control policies and research. Indeed, females should control 50% of the power.

Afrocentrism involves the process of using African principles and standards as the foundation for viewing African customs and conduct (Asante, 2009). Proponents of Afrocentrism state that African cultures and contributions have been downplayed and deliberately kept hidden under the so called *historic records*, which are controlled by Caucasians. The Afrocentrist asks what Africans would do if no Caucasians existed. Afrocentrists claim that African people are underdeveloped as a result of the a) lack of power and b) lack of control of the global economy.

According to Hall (2000), the U.S. Supreme Court's current equal protection doctrine exploits minority groups in America's increasingly multiracial society. The Supreme Court uses the image of a mosaic America to recast Caucasians as just another group that competes against other groups. By transforming Caucasians into a victim group with the same moral and legal claims as minority groups, the Court's actions fail to effectively support programs that will help minorities, such as affirmative action, while providing stronger protections for white entitlements.

Solutions to racial problems can be solved, but only if Caucasians face the fact that much of the racial problems are due to the massive crime of slavery from long ago (Dotzler, 2000). Providing the truly disadvantaged people (i.e., African Americans) with major monetary reparations will help provide minorities with the help that they need to overcome the hardships created as a result of slavery.

It is difficult to solve past injustices when the injustices continue even today. The 2003 Benton Harbor, Michigan riot is a good example of the struggle for resources and power between Caucasians and African Americans. According to Jesse Jackson, Benton Harbor's high unemployment rate, the lack of job opportunities, and the sense of hopelessness among African American residents are all believed to have been created by Caucasians (Stevens, 2003). Furthermore, the judicial system, the police, and the financial system, which are all under white control, continue to abuse African Americans.

Interpretivists argue that a person's perceptions and knowledge are shaped through lived experiences (Weber, 2004). Perceptions are shaped by individual experiences and are unique to each individual. Individuals constantly negotiate their perceptions with other people with whom they associate, reflecting an intersubjective reality.

Technical rationality supporters argue that scientific theory is more important than other theories because this theory is essential in applying theory to practice (Papell & Skolnik, 1992). Indeed, the solving of professional and complex problems depends on the general principles derived from the basic and applied sciences. However, because professional practitioners often use art and intuition to solve complex and unpredictable problems, knowledge and action, although causally connected, are inadequate in describing the competencies demonstrated by professionals. Through reflection, people obtain information that allows them to continually adapt their behaviors to overcome obstacles.

Phenomenology focuses on lived experiences and the commonalities and shared meanings in those experiences. Phenomenology explores the essence of human experience and gains a deeper understanding of an experience by uncovering hidden phenomena (Hatch, 2002; Wimpenny, Gass, & Wimpenny, 2000). Phenomenology involves the fundamental nature of reality and it questions what can really be known about it (Ponterotto, 2005). Because people are an integral part of the environment and each person has his or her own human experiences and perspectives, reality is co-created with other individuals.

Hermeneutics study the interpretation of both verbal and nonverbal forms of communication. Hermeneutics interpret life's events through lived experiences and language (Dowling, 2004). Supporters of hermeneutics believe that investigators have biases that play an essential part in the evidence collection, analysis, and interpretation processes because the biases may serve as reference (Ponterotto, 2005). This will allow the investigator to effectively probe individuals for further information during an interview process, perhaps in the form of examples. In short, it is believed that these biases will improve an investigator's understanding of the information received from individuals (Dowling). However, because everyone has different lived experiences, each person will develop a different truth (Chessick, 1990). Indeed, two investigators may evaluate the same information and may arrive at two different conclusions.

Ethnography seeks to describe a culture from the local or indigenous people's point of view (Berg, 2007). Data collection includes participant observation, participant interviewing, and artifact examination in order "to understand the cultural knowledge that group members use to make sense of the everyday experiences" (Hatch, 2002, p. 21). Examining the writings and the types of markers used in gravesites are examples of collecting artifact data. See *Table 1* for different lenses of truth.

Table 1
Different Lenses of Truth

Lens	Beliefs
Positivists	World is ordered and reality is something to be captured, studied, and understood
Logical positivists	An objective reality exists and is independent of human mind and human behavior
Post positivists	Reality exists but cannot be fully understood or realized due to limited human intelligence
Post modernists	Everything in life that is perceived is conditioned by culture, interactions, and institutions. Life's events occur by chance and, although humans are role-makers, their roles are unstable constructions

Constructivists	Reject scientific realism and argue that there are multiple subjective realities and that absolute realities are unknowable
Post structuralists	There is no truth and order is created within an individual's mind in order to give meaning to the universe
Pragmatists	Truth is defined by what is effective, useful, and brings about positive consequences
Critical theorists and feminists	World consists of historically situated structures that have a real impact on the lives of individuals based on race, social class, and gender; knowledge is subjective and political
Afrocentrism	Uses African principles and standards as the foundation for viewing African customs and conduct; asks what Africans would do if no Caucasians existed
Interpretivists	A person's perceptions and knowledge are shaped through lived experiences
Technical rationalist	Scientific theory is more important than other theories because scientific theory is essential in applying theory to practice
Phenomenologist	Explores the essence of experience and gains a deeper understanding of an experience by uncovering hidden phenomena; reality is co-created with other individuals
Hermeneutics	Interprets life's events through lived experiences and language; because everyone has different lived experiences, each person develops a different truth
Ethnography	Describes a culture from the local or indigenous people's point of view

Paradigms of American Society

The four major paradigms, or theoretical perspectives, dominating American sociological thinking are a) **functionalism and the systems paradigm**, b) **interactionism and the conduct paradigm**, c) **critical theory and the conflict paradigm**, and d) **exchange theory and ecological perspective** (Straus, 2002). The **functionalism and the systems paradigm** states that the properties of a society are based on the interrelatedness of its members and not on the individual characteristics of the members themselves. The **interactionism and the conduct paradigm** states that people interact with one another in determining their realities. The **critical theory and the conflict paradigm** state that social conditions are influenced through group conflicts. The **exchange theory and ecological perspective** states that social conditions are influenced through interpersonal and intergroup transactions. Thus, all four paradigms dominate contemporary American sociology, they all involve the interaction between society's members, and they all help make practical sense of everyday life.

The Functionalism and the Systems Paradigm

The functionalism and the systems paradigm states that society has functional needs and that the form of society will change to meet those needs (Straus, 2002). According to this paradigm, society is a cohesive system and members are naturally integrated into systems so that they can work for the common good of the whole. In other words, social behaviors contribute toward the well-being of society and a healthy society is one of harmonious equilibrium.

The Interactionism and the Conduct Paradigm

The interactionism and the conduct paradigm states that human conduct is self-conscious and self-directed (Straus, 2002). According to this paradigm, human behaviors are influenced by social rules and this is what distinguishes human behavior from other biological creatures. Furthermore, human beings interact through symbolic communication and, consequently, they socially construct reality. In addition, this paradigm assumes that social members start life about equal, it downplays the impact of larger social factors, it assumes that social order is based on mutual conspiracy, and it assumes that society as a whole buys into it. This paradigm directly challenges the functionalism and the systems paradigm.

The Critical Theory and the Conflict Paradigm

The critical theory and the conflict paradigm states that conflict is the result of power differentials and resource allocation, it is universal, and it strongly influences a person's relationship to society (Straus, 2002). On the one hand, conflict can be destructive and can escalate into social disputes. On the other hand, conflict can promote social cohesiveness through problem resolution. According to this paradigm, conflict is a fact of social life and the manner in which it is handled will influence social relationships. Furthermore, this perspective challenges the functionalism and the systems paradigm by claiming that there is nothing natural or necessary about economic inequality.

The Exchange Theory and Ecological Perspective

Unlike the functionalism and the systems paradigm that focuses on the needs of society, the exchange theory and ecological perspective states that technology, population characteristics, and the physical environment are the primary factors of social organization (Straus, 2002). According to this paradigm, social life is based on interpersonal and intergroup transactions involving social, physical, and biological factors in which each person attempts to maximize personal gain. By having accepted norms that govern fair trade, competition can be realized without conflict.

Deviance

Deviance is described as the source of innovation that results when a person takes one measurable step away from the normally accepted policies and attacks the status quo (Perkins, 2002). Deviance is an innovation virus that attacks traditional thinking at the core level. Furthermore, a person's culture may impact what the person defines as deviant.

In order to evaluate what is normal behavior and what is deviant behavior, some reference point is needed (Liska & Messner, 1999). Consequently, different interest groups struggle for power and the group that comes out on top, the dominate group, establishes what is considered to be normal behavior. Some actions are guided by what is defined as

28

proper (acceptable) social etiquette and cultural customs, and some are defined by laws. Although many people may violate accepted cultural customs of etiquette during their lives, this is considered normal if the behaviors are not continued for prolonged periods of time. If the behaviors are practiced over prolonged periods of time, then those people are labeled as social deviants.

Some rules are considered serious enough to write down and to enforce, punishing those individuals who do not conform to the specified guidelines. However, laws are not universally and evenly applied to all persons (Liska & Messner, 1999). Even though law enforcement officers know that certain persons commit crimes, charges are not always filed. Even if charges are filed, there is a good chance that prosecutors will dismiss some of the cases for one reason or another (caseload, personal acquaintance, etc.). Finally, even if a person is arrested and convicted of a crime, there is no consistency in sentencing. Outside factors, such as jail space availability, the status of the convicted person within the community, and the community's reaction to the conviction may all affect a judge's decision on a case-by-case basis.

Ethical Systems: What is Good Behavior?

Ethics is the study of human conduct in the light of set ideas of right and wrong (i.e., morals) (Pollock, 2004). However, there are different ideas of right and wrong in which to judge good behavior. Consequently, different ethical systems answer the question, "What is good?" in different manners. **Moral principles** are set ideas of right and wrong that form the basis of ethical behaviors.

Deontological ethical system is concerned with the intent of the actor or goodwill as the element of morality (Pollock, 2004). The consequence of the action is unimportant. For example, the assassination of Hitler might be unethical under a deontological system because killing is always wrong. For police officers, lying to a serial killer to get a confession is unethical because lying is intentional deceit (deceit is not goodwill).

Teleological ethical system is concerned with the consequences of an action to determine goodness (Pollock, 2004). For example, the assassination of Hitler might be ethical under a teleological system because the consequence may save many lives. For police officers, lying to a serial killer to get a confession is ethical because it may save innocent lives in the future.

Each ethical system answers the question, "What is good?" In other words, good behavior is relative and depends on the reference system (i.e., morals) used to judge behavior. For example, a behavior may be considered good according to one ethical system and bad according to another ethical system. However, not all behaviors are subject to ethical judgment; only those behaviors that are performed by humans acting with free will and that impact other people are subject to ethical judgment. In addition, a particular act may be defined as bad behavior for one person but not bad behavior for another person. For example, a child under the age of reason and a person that is mentally incapacitated may lack the knowledge and intent of wrong doing. Therefore, good behavior is relative. In addition, although personal values may influence individual moral beliefs and behaviors, not all personal values have ethical components. For example, the act of valuing one color automobile over another is ethically neutral and is based solely on personal opinion.

Different criteria are used to decide what is right or wrong. There are various ethical systems that use different criteria to evaluate the morality of an action. An action that may be considered moral by one ethical system may be considered immoral according to the standards of another ethical system. For example, although some people may go out of their way to kill spiders and think nothing of it, others may view such acts as cruelty to animals and they may demand criminal punishment. Some of the basic ethical systems that shape moral and ethical principles include a) ethical formalism, b) utilitarianism c) act utilitarianism, d) rule utilitarianism, e) religious ethics, f) natural law, g) ethics of virtue, h) ethics of care , i) egoism, j) enlightened egoism, k) ethical relativism, l) cultural relativism, and m) situational ethics (Pollock, 2004).

Ethical formalism ethical system states that good is defined by a person's goodwill and by doing one's duty (Pollock, 2004). Good actions are based on categorical imperatives: a) act as if the behavior will become a universal law, b) do not use people for one's own purposes, and c) act consistent with universal laws. For example, a lie is only a lie if the recipient is led to believe or has a right to believe that he or she is being told the truth. For instance, not telling a car thief that a bait car is being used to capture car thieves is not unethical. However, ethical formalism is problematic when there are conflicting duties (e.g., a judge's order versus department policy).

Utilitarianism ethical system determines good by a benefit-to-cost ratio (Kraska, 2004; Pollock, 2004). The needs of the many outweigh the needs of the few. For example, it is okay to arrest innocent people by mistake if it solves a bigger problem.

Act Utilitarianism ethical system determines the goodness of a particular act by measuring the utility of the specific act without regard for future acts (Pollock, 2004). For example, it may be ethical to steal food when a person is hungry and has no other way to get food because acting in a way that prevents a person from starving to death is deemed as good.

Rule Utilitarianism ethical system determines the goodness of an action by measuring the utility of the action when made into a rule for behavior (Pollock, 2004). For example, it is unethical to steal food when a person is hungry and has no other way to get food because this will result in lawlessness if people are allowed to steal food anytime that they are hungry and cannot afford food. Also, it may be unethical for police not to engage in high speed car chases because police not pursuing violators may encourage people to flee (no chase policies may enhance the problem).

Religious ethics ethical system determines the goodness of an action based on the concepts of good and evil, which are defined by the will of God (Pollock, 2004). Ethics are determined by individual conscious, religious authorities, and Holy Scripture. However, problems with religious ethics include a) no one may ever know exactly the will of God and b) there are current controversies within and between religions. For example, it may not be unethical or illegal for Native Americans to consume contraband mushrooms during religious services.

Natural law ethical system states that there is a universal set of rights and wrongs but without reference to specific supernatural beings (Pollock, 2004). What is good is determined by what is natural to humans (e.g., socialization and right to life) and is free of passion. Indeed, the founding fathers might be described as natural law practitioners. However, identifying what is consistent and congruent with natural inclinations of humankind is a fundamental problem of this ethical system. This is evident by the fact that some laws have changed over time and new laws are continually being developed.

Ethics of virtue ethical system determines the goodness of an action based on the attempt to achieve happiness, such as living a good life and achieving life's goals (Pollock, 2004). Good behavior is based on the golden mean, which is the median between extreme states of character. For example, absolute police powers and civil liberties oppose one another. Effective law enforcement must compromise between the two. It is based on a person's character and includes factors such as honesty, humility, and temperance.

Ethics of care ethical system determines the goodness of an action based on meeting needs and preserving and enriching relationships (Pollock, 2004). Good actions are based on connecting with other people, caring for the needs of other people, and being aware of other people. For example, if a police officer sees a threatening argument, instead of arresting the violator for intimidation (a felony), the police officer may arrest the violator for disorderly conduct (a misdemeanor), provocation (a civil infraction), or simply separate the parties and give the violator a warning. By taking the minimum enforcement action necessary to achieve peace, relationships will be enhanced and labeling may be prevented.

Egoism ethical system claims that good actions promote self-interests (Pollock, 2004). However, it is not logical or feasible that all people act in their own best interests because this will result in great conflict. Indeed, laws are designed to control behavior and to promote safety. People are expected to obey the law even if it is not always profitable to them (e.g., pay taxes).   In law enforcement, when a quota is used to judge an officer's performance, meeting the quota becomes more important than doing the right thing.

Enlightened egoism claims that it is one's long-term best interest to help others so that they will learn to help themselves (Pollock, 2004). For example, a police officer may refuse to change a flat tire on a car that is occupied by capable adults. Instead, the officer may instruct the occupants on how to change the tire themselves. This may help the occupants if they get a flat tire in the future. However, community members may expect the police to provide full and immediate service and this may result in complaints. In order to prevent complaints, a police officer in the field may offer full service by providing wrecker service (the officer still did not change the tire). This may damage police-community relations.

Ethical relativism ethical system determines what is good or bad based on the individual or group (Pollock, 2004). For example, community members in a poor region may hunt and fish without purchasing the proper licenses. Also, prostitution may be encouraged and institutionalized in certain societies.

Cultural relativism defines good as that which contributes to the health and survival of society (Pollock, 2004). For example, women in certain cultures will wear covers and they will not expose their faces to strange men (if they do, their husbands may kill them). This may promote family relations within a society, which may promote health of the society. However, this may be problematic for U.S. law enforcement officers, who are often required to identify individuals. For example, U.S. Customs & Border Protection officers are required to identify individuals coming into the U.S. If individuals refuse to show their faces, and if U.S. law enforcement officers are required to see their faces, conflict may develop.

Situational ethics ethical system states that there are few universal truths and that different situations call for different responses (Pollock, 2004). Thus, the same action may be right in some situations and wrong in other situations. For example, it may be ethical for a person to violate the speed laws if he or she is racing an injured person to the hospital. However, the same action may be unethical if no such emergency exists. See *Figure 2* for a summary of the ethical systems.

The Question of Deceiving Suspects: Is it <u>Justified</u> for Police to Lie?

Answer: It depends on the perspective one takes!

Ethical Formalism: condemned, due to violation of categorical imperative; lying would become rule for all people

Utilitarianism: justified, if benefits outweigh costs to society as a whole

Religion: condemned, due to lying; God is truth

Natural Law: justified, as long as civil rights are not violated

Ethics of Virtue: justified, if crimes are severe and if methods are moderate

Ethics of Care: justified, if it protects the victim (not justified for victimless crimes)

Egoism: justified, if profitable to officer (e.g., performance evaluation)

Act Utilitarianism: justified, if benefits outweigh costs of methods employed (crime dependent)

Rule Utilitarianism: condemned because it may undermine the long term system of laws

Enlightened Egoism: justified, if long term benefits are greater than loss of trust in police

Cultural Relativism: justified, as long as accepted by culture

Situational Ethics: justified, if police officer can articulate reasons for deception

Ethics in Law Enforcement

Utilitarianism

Good is based on a benefit-cost ratio. Example of good behavior: arresting an innocent person in order to deter crime in general.

Types of Ethical Systems

- Ethical Formalism
- Utilitarianism
- Religious
- Natural Law
- Ethics of Virtue
- Ethics of Care
- Egoism
- Cultural Relativism
- Situational Ethics

Ethics in Law Enforcement

What is good behavior?

Ethics is the study of set ideas of right and wrong. However, there are different ideas of right and wrong in which to judge good behavior. Consequently, different ethical systems answer the question, "What is good?" in different manners.

Religious

Good is based on God's will. Example of good behavior: always providing complete and truthful information, regardless of the cost.

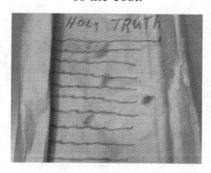

Ethical Formalism

Good is based on goodwill and intent. Example of good behavior: catching a fleeing felon, even if the violator gets hurt.

Figure 2. Types of Ethical Systems.

Ethics in Law Enforcement

Natural Law

Good is based on a universal set of rights (i.e., what is natural).

Example of good behavior: acting in accordance with the U.S. Constitution.

Ethics of Care

Good is based on the needs of those concerned.

Example of good behavior: always arresting males who are involved in domestic violence in order to protect female victims.

Cultural Relativism

Good is based on what promotes the health and survival of society.

Example of good behavior: Middle Eastern women refusing to show their faces in public.

Ethics of Virtue

Good is based on compromise.

Example of good behavior: using non-intrusive X-Ray machines to search for contraband.

X-Ray

Egoism

Good is based on what benefits the actor.

Example of good behavior: writing a lot of tickets to meet the monthly quota for a good performance review.

Tickets	257
Warnings	33
Misd. Arrests	7
Felony Arrests	3
DUI Arrests	4

Situational Ethics

Good is based on the particular situation at a particular time.

Example of good behavior: speeding in order to get to the hospital to save a life.

Figure 2 (continued). Types of Ethical Systems.

Summary of Ethical Systems

Good Behavior

- Morals – set of ideas of right and wrong according to socio-cultural environment

- Ethics- study of human conduct in light of morals

- What is defined as good may be relative if considering other viewpoints

Types of Ethical Systems

- Ethical Formalism (good intentions)

- Utilitarianism (benefit-cost ratio)

- Religious (God's will)

- Natural Law (natural; U.S. Constitution)

- Ethics of Virtue (compromise)

- Ethics of care (needs of those concerned)

- Egoism (personal gain)

- Cultural Relativism (promotes health of society)

- Situational Ethics (unique to situation)

Example – Police Lying to Suspect - Is it good behavior?

- Ethical Formalism (yes for society, no for suspect)

- Utilitarianism (yes, if benefit > cost; no, if benefit < cost)

- Religious (no)

- Natural Law (yes, as allowed by law)

- Ethics of Virtue (yes, if justice is served; no, if nothing is gained)

- Ethics of care (yes, if it helps someone involved; no, if no one involved is helped)

- Egoism (yes, for the officer - if it promotes personal gain; no, for the suspect)

- Cultural Relativism (depends on society's belief – if it promotes social health)

- Situational Ethics (depends if it is necessary to meet a greater goal)

Point of View- Exercise

Read the following paragraph. Highlight important information as if you are the individual who enters the home and you are *a burglar*.

An individual enters a home. Outside the home there are surveillance cameras. Inside the home, there is a strong odor of mold in the air. There is a 70" flat-screen TV and a laptop in the living room. In the kitchen there is a backed-up sink and the pipe is leaking. Near the sink are a woman's diamond ring and a gold watch. There is a desk in the study, which has a large amount of cash resting on it. There is also a permanent wall-mounted safe in one of the closets. In one of the bedrooms comes the sound of someone snoring. In the same bedroom, water is dripping from the ceiling.   You hear the sound of a car outside as it pulls into the driveway.

Read the following paragraph. Highlight important information as if you are the individual who enters the home and you are *a potential home buyer*.

An individual enters a home. Outside the home there are surveillance cameras. Inside the home, there is a strong odor of mold in the air. There is a 70" flat-screen TV and a laptop in the living room. In the kitchen there is a backed-up sink and the pipe is leaking. Near the sink are a woman's diamond ring and a gold watch. There is a desk in the study, which has a large amount of cash resting on it. There is also a permanent wall-mounted safe in one of the closets. In one of the bedrooms comes the sound of someone snoring. In the same bedroom, water is dripping from the ceiling.   You hear the sound of a car outside as it pulls into the driveway.

How does having a different purpose and perspective change the way you evaluate the information provided?

Police Department Orientation & Criminal Justice Purpose

Eight theoretical orientations have been identified that describe the lenses through which police department administrators perceive crime and the criminal justice system (Kraska, 2004). See *Figure 3*. The orientation that a police department follows will influence how patrol officers act toward the public. The eight orientations include a) Rational, b) System, c) Crime Control versus Due Process, d) Politics and Criminal Justice, e) Growth Complex, f) Social Constructionist, g) Oppression, and h) Late Modernity. Each of these orientations is based on different assumptions. Although there are different ethical systems to judge good behavior, police officers are also judged by the police department's orientation. An officer may experience conflict if the police department's orientation is not in alignment with what the public expects to be the practiced ethical system.

Rational Orientation

The rational/legal orientation simply views law enforcement as a business. Peace and security can be achieved by controlling crime, and crime can be controlled by punishing offenders (Kraska, 2004). In other words, everyone is expected to follow the rules in order to achieve the agreed upon end result, which is peace. When a man, for example, decides not to follow the rules, he creates a tear in the fabric of peace, and this fabric must be repaired, which requires a cost. By not following the rules, this man has encroached upon the rights of other individuals and is forcing them to pay a cost for which he is responsible. Because this is not fair, laws are required to balance things out; the offender must pay a cost high enough, not only to repair the damage, but to deter him from disrupting social order in the future. If the penalty only matches the cost of repair and is not high enough to discourage future acts of deviance, then the person would be just as likely to commit crimes as to follow the rules, which would undermine public confidence in public safety. The greater the cost is to the public, the greater the cost that must be paid by the offender.

The main assumptions of the rational/legal choice orientation are that everyone in society has equal value, everyone is in alignment, and everyone concedes to follow the agreed upon rules. It assumes that everyone has given up a little bit of personal freedom so that the government can enforce the agreed upon rules in order to promote public safety in a fair and impartial manner (Kraska, 2004). It assumes that crime has a cost and can be managed through payment.

System Orientation

The system orientation views criminal justice as an entity that consists of interacting, yet independent, agencies (Kraska, 2004). The various agencies function by drawing inputs from the external environment, transforming these inputs, and then sending the final product back into the environment as socially approved output. An example would be to collect convicts (input), to rehabilitate them through behavior modification programs (transform), and then to release them back into society (output). The system's independent units strive to maintain balance and internal stability as they sustain each other. It is believed that crime is a rational choice and that the size and power of the system must be increased in order to accommodate increases in the crime rate.

The primary purpose of the criminal justice system, according to the system orientation, is controlling crime (Kraska, 2004). It is believed that public safety can be achieved through efficient operations of each unit of the criminal justice system, including legislative, executive, judicial, and correctional agencies. In this way, accused persons can be processed, rehabilitated, and returned to society in an effective and efficient manner that promotes social peace.

The main assumptions of the system orientation are that those who have legal authority are capable of making rational decisions, which will reduce crime in an efficient manner (Kraska, 2004). It is believed that the system can adapt itself to accommodate changes in the external environment, usually by increasing its resources. By effectively and

41

efficiently using resources and technology, by improving laws and policies, by improving judicial processes, and by improving rehabilitation and re-entry programs, it is expected that crime can be better controlled and public safety will be enhanced.

Crime Control versus Due Process Orientation

The main purpose of the **crime control orientation** is to secure peace by arresting as many law violators as possible, as fast as possible, and by using as few resources per arrest as possible (Kraska, 2004). Furthermore, because the defendants are presumed guilty (otherwise they would not have been arrested), releasing suspects due to procedural mistakes is wrong. In other words, suspects are guilty of their alleged crimes, otherwise law enforcement authorities would not spend the resources trying to prosecute the person (i.e., effective crime control does not focus on innocent people). It is believed that this quantitative based tough-on-crime policy can be achieved by efficiently processing offenders informally and consistently through the legal system; this requires having few constitutional restraints placed upon law enforcers. However, the crime control orientation assumes that law enforcers a) are trustworthy and will enforce laws in a fair and legal manner, and b) can competently reconstruct crime scenes and develop the most accurate account of the actual events in a descriptive and factual manner. In short, mistakes are tolerated up to the point where they start to interfere with the suppression of crime.

The main purpose of the **due process orientation** is to protect people's rights by placing constraints upon the government and by making government officials defend their investigative procedures in an adversarial courtroom (Kraska, 2004). Due process advocates believe that mistakes are unacceptable, individual freedom is more valuable than absolute security, and that factual guilt does not equate to legal guilt. However, unless a person is provided the opportunity to present evidence, it is assumed that this distinction will not be made. This qualitative based policy assumes that the defendant will be provided adequate legal representation in the courtroom and that the legal system will lead to the discovery of the truth (i.e., whether the police honored procedural safeguards, as guaranteed by law). Indeed, due process orientation requires that an unbiased third party (i.e., the judge or jury) make an objective evaluation of legal guilt.

Due process advocates view criminal justice as a necessary means to protect social freedom by protecting all citizens from unjust acts committed by government officials (Kraska, 2004). Because the cost of being incarcerated is extremely high, the due process orientation requires that the state eliminate all doubt as to whether constitutional procedural safeguards were followed. In order to control law enforcers, there must be a cost for violating the rules. Thus, in order to ensure that police officers will comply with the law, it is argued that the cost of releasing all suspects whose rights have been violated will be a high enough cost to motivate law enforcers to obey the law when they perform their duties. Corrupt police officers will cause the crime control orientation to fail.

Politics and Criminal Justice Orientation

According to the politics orientation, the criminal justice system is interest based and its primary purpose is contingent on the political climate at the time (Kraska, 2004). However, the political climate continually changes because it depends on the interest groups that have political power. Many interests groups fight for power and want to protect their own self-interests. Through negotiations, the different groups can protect their own interests through checks and balances. This promotes an orderly offender processing system via rational policies. Politics has two sides, a right wing and a left wing.

The right wing is conservative and the left wing is liberal (Kraska, 2004). On the one hand, the right wing believes that a) the system is too lenient with offenders, b) the system favors the rights of the offenders over the rights of victims, c) youths no longer respect authorities, d) hard working law-abiding Americans are paying the high cost for crime, and e) society is too permissive involving morality issues. The left wing, on the other hand, believes that a) the system inappropriately includes certain vices as crimes, which indicates a more serious crime problem than really exists, b) authorities label people as criminals, which may stigmatize them and create a self-fulfilling prophecy, c) correctional facilities warehouse criminals and fail to rehabilitate them, which leads to recidivism, d) centralized power discourages the involvement of community members in solving local problems, and e) the criminal justice system discriminates against and segregates minorities in order to control them.

The right wing and the left wing each have their own set of assumptions (Kraska, 2004). The right wing's assumptions state that a) people are responsible for their own actions, b) strong morals, based on a religious foundation, are essential for a healthy and well-functioning society, c) people have the right to be safe and secure in the areas where they spend most of their time, d) a healthy society requires that people obey the law, which will be administered fairly and firmly, and e) social order requires that major categories of persons be segregated so that they can be controlled. The left wing's assumptions state that a) the primary cause of crime lies in dysfunctional social conditions, b) obsolete morality regulations are deficient in meeting the current needs of a majority of the population, c) there is an unequal distribution of power and resources in the country, d) a healthy society cannot discriminate against major categories of persons, e) official authorities stigmatize offenders by labeling them as criminals, which will lead to hardship and future crime, and f) the crime problem is exaggerated (thus, legal codes should be changed so that victimless crimes are not counted toward the crime problem).

Growth Complex Orientation

According to the growth complex orientation, the purpose of the criminal justice system is to build an ever growing bureaucracy; administering justice and controlling crime are tools that are used to increase the agency's size and power (Kraska, 2004). In an effort to meet the organizational ends in the most efficient way, scientific methods are established in order to create rules and regulations, which will get everyone to perform their duties in the same technically efficient and predictable manner. Instead of focusing on the outcome (doing the right thing), the rules and regulations become the standard for performance.

44

Police departments use statistics to defend their enforcement practices. When someone challenges their apparently unfair enforcement tactics, the police can claim that individuals are arrested based on objective numeric analysis. They may also argue that without using statistics to classify and sentence people, each person's fate would be inconsistent and uncertain. Furthermore, part of the criminal justice system has become privatized, and many investors hope to profit (Kraska, 2004). On the one hand, the investors create many jobs. For example, workers are needed to build prisons, supply prison food, supply prison clothes, and provide medical care. On the other hand, the investors need customers (i.e., inmates); hence, there is an incentive to confine people in prison. By locking people up in prison, the state effectively manages the surplus labor force, which is naturally generated in a capitalistic society (Kraska, 2004). Thus, politicians appear to be effectively serving the public. After all, jobs are created and there are fewer unemployed people in the marketplace.

The main assumptions of the growth complex orientation are that a) a bureaucracy needs to survive and grow, b) people desire to build dynasties that extend their power and create a type of immorality, c) the use of rational and efficient methods are the best way to measure performance, d) capitalism and efficiency take precedence over human dignity (consequently, people lose sight of their morals), e) a matrix of organizations, interests, and resources is needed for growth, f) punishing people is good financial business and creates many jobs, and g) profiteers are not held accountable for their faulty products and their low quality services.

Social Constructionist Orientation

The social constructionist orientation is based upon interpretivism, which has both subjective and objective qualities (Kraska, 2004). On the one hand, interpretivism is subjective and claims that reality and meanings are shaped via individual experiences, which are unique to each individual. On the other hand, interpretivism is objective and claims that individuals constantly negotiate their perceptions with other people with whom

45

they associate, reflecting an intersubjective reality (Weber, 2004). Indeed, there is no one single truth; reality for each person is constructed relative to personal experiences based upon language, symbols, and the interactions with other individuals (Kraska).

According to the social constructionist orientation, the purpose of the criminal justice system is socially constructed and depends on the political climate, social sentiment, cultural values, intellectual perspectives, and interests of those in power (Kraska, 2004). By using the media to manage the appearance of the system's legitimacy, the public is continually bombarded with myths until the myths become accepted as facts. The criminal justice system can provide the public with select information, which creates the perception that the status quo must be maintained. Police can effectively create their own jobs by persuading the public to support their current efforts.

The assumptions of the social constructionist orientation are a) the police use myths to develop problems that do not really exist, which divert public attention away from the real problems in society (e.g., unemployment and discrimination), and b) the interests of people in power must be protected (Kraska, 2004). Using the media, who need exciting crime stories to sell their product, the police can provide the information needed to create moral panic. By appearing to effectively react to a problem, which never really existed, the police gain the public's support.

Late Modernity Orientation

According to the late modernity orientation, the purpose of the criminal justice system is to promote safety and security by effectively identifying and managing classes of people who have been assessed as threats (Kraska, 2004). The "goal is not to eliminate crime but to make it tolerable through systematic coordination" (Kraska, p. 305-307). Late modernity is not concerned with the underlying causes of crime; rather, it uses statistics to assess risk levels of particular classes of people and then tries to control populations that are identified as high risk. By incarcerating the high risk groups of people, significant aggregate effects in crime can be realized. In other words, crime can be reduced by rearranging the type of people who are still out in the general population (i.e., it reduces the percentage of high risk people who are roaming around in free society).

The main assumptions of the late modernity orientation are that state cannot provide effective overall security, that private persons need to invest in their own situational crime prevention programs, and that people rationally choose to commit crime (Kraska, 2004). Because situational crime prevention programs require financial resources to implement, this excludes many of the poor people (who end up being labeled as outsiders). Late modernity orientation supporters claim that these misfortunate people are responsible for their own fates. By classifying these misfortunate individuals as outsiders, the dominant classes can effectively control them without the dominant classes giving up their own freedoms. Indeed, authorities can effectively control these misfortunate people because incarceration is easy to implement, it results in immediate consequence, it has few political opponents, it relies on the existing system of regulations, and it leaves the fundamental social and economic systems intact.

Oppression Orientation

Oppression orientation claims that the state protects the interests of the elite and powerful while oppressing the disadvantaged and less powerful (Kraska, 2004). In other words, the state uses the law as a tool for the political repression of those groups that threaten state power. There is a struggle for power and the groups that attain the most power are the ones that dictate what is considered illegal. According to the oppression orientation, the purpose of the criminal justice system is to control people who threaten the status quo. Those who are less powerful politically, which includes minorities, women, and the poor, are used as scapegoats for America's problems. By using scapegoats, society is able to overlook the underlying factors that actually cause significant social harm (e.g., unemployment and poverty).

Police Department Orientations

Crime Control

The overall goal is to control crime by arresting as many people as possible as fast as possible. Mistakes are acceptable; police are trustworthy and they only arrest the guilty.

Police Department Orientations

- **Rational**
- **Crime Control**
- **Due Process**
- **System**
- **Politics and Criminal Justice**
- **Growth Complex**
- **Social Constructionist**
- **Late Modernity**
- **Oppression**

Police Department Orientations

What is good police officer behavior?

Police managers have different ideas of right and wrong in which to judge good police officer behavior. Consequently, different police department orientations answer the question, "What is good police officer behavior?" in different manners.

Due Process

Personal freedom is more valuable than absolute security. People have a right to legal representation; police need to prove case in court. Mistakes by the police are unacceptable.

Rational

Law enforcement is a business. Everyone agrees to give up some freedom for peace and security. If the cost for crime is high enough, individuals will rationally choose to obey the law.

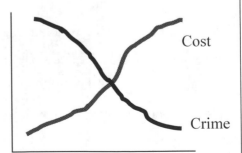

Cost

Crime

Figure 3. Police Department Orientations.

Police Department Orientations

System

Independent agencies work together to collect deviants, to transform them, and to return them to society. Public safety can be achieved through inter-agency cooperation and efficient operation of each agency.

Growth Complex

Purpose of police is to build an ever growing bureaucracy. Police rules become the standard to measure performance (quotas). Police create problems to ensure jobs. Human dignity is unimportant; punishing individuals is profitable.

Late Modernity

Purpose of police is to use statistics to assess risk levels and to promote safety by controlling the classes of people who have been identified as the problem. Individuals need to take responsibility to protect themselves.

Crime Rate of Targeted Class

Politics and Criminal Justice

Purpose of police depends on who has political power. Right wing: system is too lenient; left wing: system is too controlling.

Social Constructionist

Purpose of police is based on interpretivism. Good behavior is determined by culture, by social sentiment, and by people in power. Because there is no single truth, police use media to create myths.

Oppression

Purpose of police is to protect the elite and powerful while controlling the disadvantaged and less powerful. The police should maintain the status quo by controlling minorities.

Figure 3 (continued). Police Department Orientations.

The assumption of oppression orientation is that the criminal justice system has built in biases against minorities, women, and the poor (Kraska, 2004). Indeed, because laws in the U.S. are based on men's perspectives, the laws are inherently biased. In short, the criminal justice system abuses its power through the practice of institutional racism, sexism, and classism. See *Figure 3* for different police department orientations.

References

Akers, R., and Sellers, C. (2009). *Criminological theories: Introduction, evaluation, and application* (5th ed.). New York, NY: Oxford University Press.

Asante, M.K. (2009). What is Afrocentricity? Retrieved on May 3, 2011 from http://www.asante.net/ scholarly/afrocentricityarticle.html

Berg, B. (2007). *Qualitative research methods for the social sciences* (6th ed.). Boston, MA: Pearson Education, Inc.

Chessick, R. (1990). Hermeneutics for psychotherapists. *American Journal of Psychotherapy, 44*(2), 256-273.

Crossan, F. (2003). Research philosophy: Towards an understanding. *Nurse Researcher, 11*(1), 46-55.

Dowling, M. (2004). Hermeneutics: An exploration. *Nurse Researcher, 11*(4), 30-39.

Dotzler, R.J. (2000). Getting to reparations: A response to Fein. *Sociological Practice: A Journal of Clinical and Applied Sociology, 2*(3), 177-182.

Glesne, C. (2006). *Becoming qualitative researchers: An introduction* (3rd ed.). Boston, MA: Pearson.

Hall, A.A. (2000). There is a lot to be repaired before we get reparations: A critique of the underlying issues of race that impact the fate of African American reparations. *St. Mary's Law Review, 1*, 22-32.

Hammers, C., and Brown, A. (2004). Towards a feminist-queer alliance: A paradigmatic shift in the research process. *Social Epistemology, 18*(1).

Hatch, J. (2002). *Doing qualitative research in education settings*. Albany, NY: State University of New York Press.

Holliday, A. (2007). *Doing and writing qualitative research* (2nd ed.). Thousand Oaks, CA: Sage.

Kraska, P. (2004). *Theorizing criminal justice: Eight essential orientations*. Long Grove, IL: Waveland Press, Inc.

Liska, A. and Messner, S. (1999). *Perspectives on Crime and Deviance* (3rd ed.). Upper Saddle River, NJ: Prentice Hall.

McLaughlin, E., & Muncie, J. (2006). *The Sage dictionary of criminology* (2nd ed.). Thousand Oaks, CA: Sage.

Mertens, D.M. (2005). *Research and evaluation in education and psychology: integrating diversity with quantitative, qualitative, and mixed methods* (2nd ed.). Thousand Oaks, CA: Sage Publications.

Papell, C., and Skolnik, L. (1992). The reflective practitioner: A contemporary paradigm's relevance for social work education. *Journal of Social Work Education, 28*(1), 18-26.

Perkins, C. (2002). In support of deviance. *ID, 38*(4).

Pollock, J.M. (2004). *Ethics in crime and justice: Dilemmas & decisions*. Belmont, CA: Thomas-Wadsworth.

Ponterotto, J. (2005). Qualitative research in counseling psychology: A primer on research paradigms and philosophy of science. *Journal of Counseling, 52*(2), 126-136.

Schmalleger, F. (2007). *Criminal justice today: An introductory text for the 21ˢᵗ century* (9th ed.). Upper Saddle River, NJ: Pearson Prentice Hall.

Straus, R. (2002). Using sociological theory to make practical sense out of social life. In R. Straus (Ed.), *Using sociology: An introduction from the applied and clinical perspectives* (3rd ed.) (p. 21-43). New York, NY: Rowman & Litterfield.

Weber, R. (2004). The rhetoric of positivism versus interpretivism: A personal view. *MIS Quarterly, 28*(1), iii-xii.

Wimpenny, P., Gass, J., & Wimpenny (2000). Interviewing in phenomenology and grounded theory: is there a difference? *Journal of Advanced Nursing, 31*(6), 1485-1492.

CHAPTER 3. REASONING & FLOWCHARTING

REASONING

In criminal justice, it is crucial to practice and perfect the skill of reasoning. If we operate on flawed assumptions, it could hamper our ability to successfully perform our law enforcement duties. If we act on inaccurate assumptions, it could lead to wrongful arrests or wrongful releases.

Deductive reasoning is based on drawing conclusions from statements that are accepted as true (Smith, Eggen, St. Andre, 2006). A person employing deductive reasoning will start with a general principle and will apply the information to a specific case. In other words, deductive reasoning arrives at a specific conclusion based on generalizations. Below is an example of deductive reasoning.

All apples are fruit.
All fruit grows on trees.
Therefore, all apples grow on trees.

If the initial assumptions are incorrect, then the conclusion will be flawed.

Inductive Reasoning is based on an individual making observations and then developing a generality based on those observations (Smith, Eggen, St. Andre, 2006). In other words, the observer detects patterns and then makes predictions based on those patterns. However, if the observations are proved false only one time, then the conclusions will be flawed. Below is an example of inductive reasoning.

Inductive reasoning: Predict next response.

•   ••   • • •   _____

It is easy to see how inductive reasoning can be used to predict future criminal behavior. For example, law enforcers have used inductive reasoning as a part of the totality of circumstance to profile possible terrorists. Having limited resources, police departments may try to focus their efforts on the greatest risks.

FLOWCHARTING – FOLLOWING DIRECTIONS

(*"Flow Chart"*, 2002).

Definitions of flowchart symbols.

Terminal
(start or stop)

Process
(do something)

Input or output

Decision

Flow line

Connector
(jump)

The terminal symbol indicates the starting point and ending point of the program logic flow. The process symbol is used to represent arithmetic functions and data movement instructions. The input/output symbol is used to denote any function of an input/output device. For example, data may be collected from a disk (input) or delivered to a printer (output). The decision symbol is used to indicate a point where a decision is made and there are two or more consequences. Flow lines simply provide the path of travel for the flow of operation. The on-page connector allows a point to jump elsewhere. This is useful if the flow lines become congested and start to crisscross in a particular area.

Describe the numbers that are printed in each of the programs below.

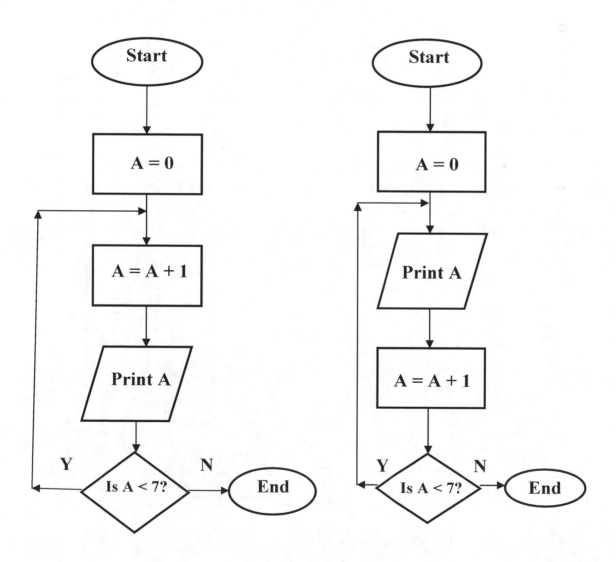

Below is a program that prints the largest of three numbers.

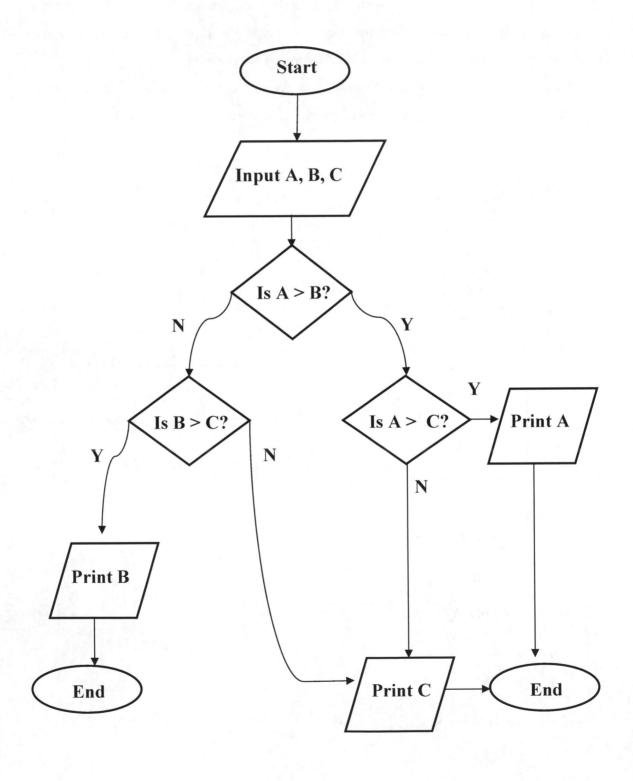

On the next page is a program in which the police select every fifth car to perform a Driving Under the Influence (DUI) investigation. The officers stopping the vehicles are on the Initial Contact Team (ICT). The officers conducting the Field Sobriety Tests are the FST Team (FSTT). (V = V+ 1 means to take the current value of V, add 1, then make that the new value of V.)

Rules:
1) The project will run for 4 hours.
2) The ICT will monitor traffic, will stop every fifth vehicle, and will administer an alco-sensor test to the driver.
3) If the alco-sensor test at initial contact is less than 0.05% BAC, then the driver will be released.
4) If the alco-sensor test at initial contact is at least 0.05% BAC, then the driver will be passed off to the Field Sobriety Test Team, who will continue the investigation via field sobriety tests (FSTs). The ICT will return to traffic.
5) If the alco-senor test is at least .05% BAC but less than .08% BAC, and if the driver passes the FSTs, then the FSTT will release the driver.
6) If the alco-sensor test at initial contact is at least 0.08% BAC, then the driver will automatically be given a Datamaster test after the field sobriety tests.
7) If the driver fails the field sobriety tests, then the driver will be given a DataMastrer test.
8) If the DataMaster test is less than .08% BAC, and if the driver fails the FSTs, then the FSTT will charge the driver with public intoxication.
9) If the DataMaster test is at least .08% BAC, then the FSTT will charge the driver with DUI misdemeanor for the driver's first offense and DUI felony for the driver's second offense.

Driving Under the Influence (DUI) Investigation.

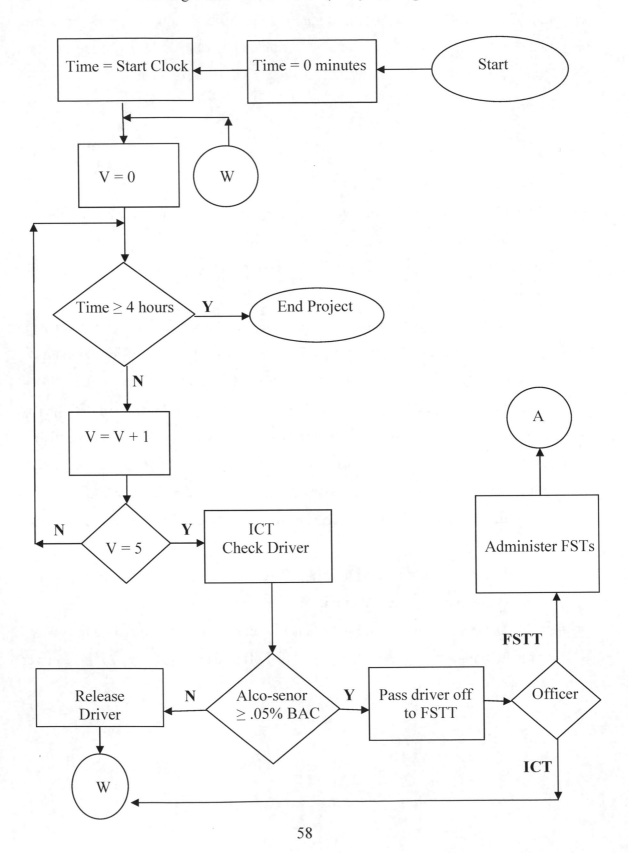

Driving Under the Influence (DUI) investigation (continued).

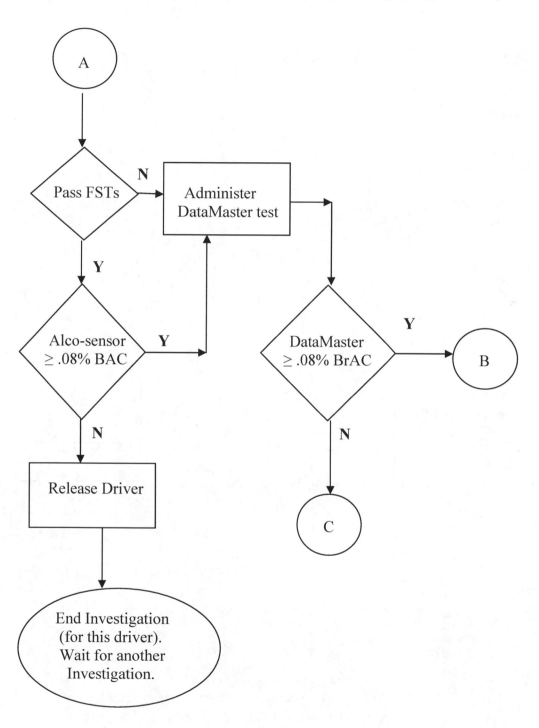

Question: How would the flowchart change if the suspect refuses the DataMaster test?

Driving Under the Influence (DUI) investigation (continued).

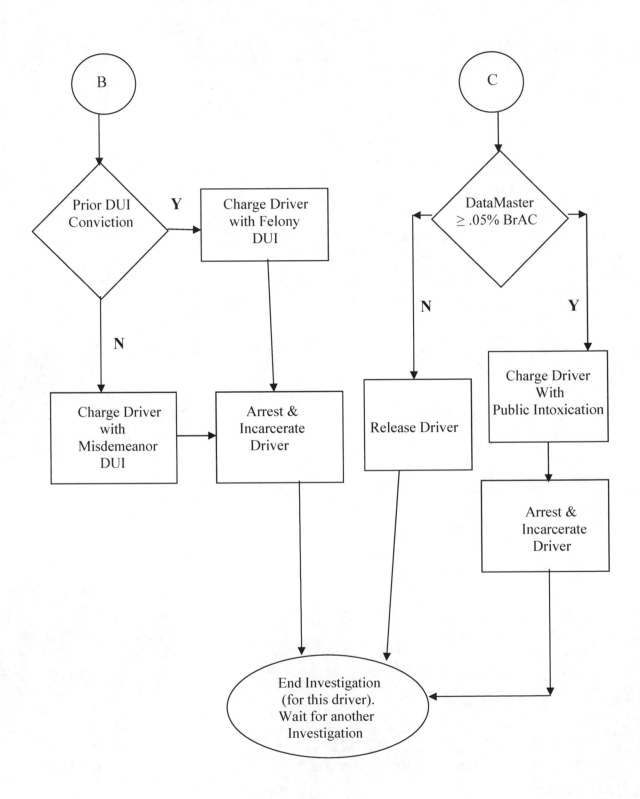

Stop and Frisk Flowchart

Below is a flowchart that explains the stop and frisk procedure. For the following flowchart, probable cause means that it is more likely than not that a crime has occurred (51% confident for practical purposes).

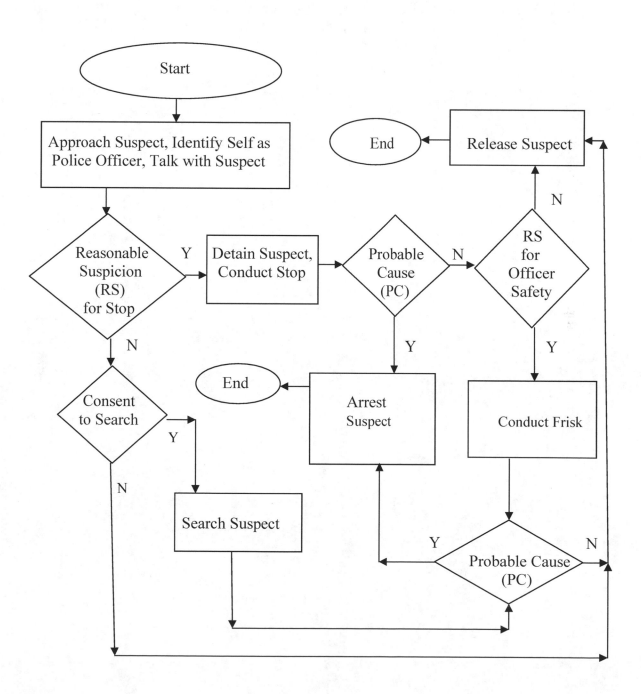

References

Flow Chart Examples (2002). Retrieved from http://elsmar.com/pdf_files/
    Flow_Charts_for_2000.pdf

Smith, S., Eggen, M., St. Andre, R. (2006). *A transition to advanced mathematics* (6th ed.).
    Belmont, CA: Thomson Brooks/Cole.

CHAPTER 4. TRUTH TABLES

(Smith, Eggen, & St. Andre, 2006).

The following exercises will require a mathematical/logical mindset. The purpose of this chapter is to challenge your problem solving skills by applying math and English to the law.

<u>Rule:</u> When sentences are presented, variables are always defined in the positive language. For example, if the law states "not intoxicated," then variable A = intoxicated (positive language) while ~ A = not intoxicated (negative language).

Number of combinations = 2^x, where x is the number of variables

Number of combinations of variables using three variables = $2^3 = 8$

∩ = And;   U = Or;   ~ = not;   **True = T = 1; False = F = 0**

If A = {0, 1, 2, 3, 4, 5}   and B = {2, 4, 7, 9},

A ∩ B = {2, 4}

and

A U B = {0, 1, 2, 3, 4, 5, 7, 9}

Examples of Truth Tables for two variables.

P	Q	P ∩ Q
T	T	T
F	T	F
T	F	F
F	F	F

P	Q	P U Q
T	T	T
F	T	T
T	F	T
F	F	F

P	~P
1	0
0	1

P	~P	~(~P)
1	0	1
0	1	0

P	Q	P ∩ Q	~(P ∩ Q)	~P	~Q	~P U ~Q	~P ∩ ~Q
T	T	T	F	F	F	F	F
F	T	F	T	T	F	T	F
T	F	F	T	F	T	T	F
F	F	F	T	T	T	T	T

Truth Tables for three variables.

R	Q	P	~P	~Q	~R	P ∩ Q	~ (P∩Q)	(P∩Q) U ~Q	PU ~Q	(PU ~Q) ∩R	~P ∩ ~Q	P ∩ ~Q
T	T	T	F	F	F	T	F	T	T	T	F	F
F	T	T	F	F	T	T	F	T	T	F	F	F
T	F	T	F	T	F	F	T	T	T	T	F	T
F	F	T	F	T	T	F	T	T	T	F	F	T
T	T	F	T	F	F	F	T	F	F	F	F	F
F	T	F	T	F	T	F	T	F	F	F	F	F
T	F	F	T	T	F	F	T	T	T	T	T	F
F	F	F	T	T	T	F	T	T	T	F	T	F

Make a truth table for each of the following propositional forms.

P ∩ P

P U ~Q

P ∩ (Q U R)

(P ∩ Q) U (P ∩ R)

P ∩ ~ Q

P ∩ (Q U ~Q)

Which pairs are equivalent (have the same truth values)?

P ∩ ~P, P

P U P, P

P U P, ~P

P U ~Q, Q ∩ ~P

P U ~Q, Q U ~ P

P U Q, Q U ~P

P ∩ Q, Q ∩ P

P ∩ ~ Q, Q ∩ ~ P

64

Make a truth table for each of the following propositional forms.

$\cap$ = And;   U = Or;   ~ = not

~ (P $\cap$ Q $\cap$ R)

~ P $\cap$ ~ Q $\cap$ ~ R

~ (P U Q U R)

~ P U ~ Q U ~ R

If P = T, Q = T, and R = F, state whether the following are true or false?

~ (P $\cap$ Q $\cap$ R)   =

~ P $\cap$ ~ Q $\cap$ ~ R   =

~ (P U Q U R)   =

~ P U ~ Q U ~ R   =

If P, Q, and R are true while S and T are false, which of the following are true?

Q $\cap$ (R $\cap$ S)

Q U (R $\cap$ S)

(P U Q) $\cap$ (R U S)

Q U (R $\cap$ S)

(P U Q) $\cap$ (R U S)

[(~ P) U (~ Q)] U [(~ R) U (~ S)]

Which combination of variables (laws) are equivalent (i.e., have the same truth values)?

R	Q	P	~P	~Q	~R	P∩Q∩R	~(P∩Q∩R)	~P∩~Q∩~R	P∪Q∪R	~(P∪Q∪R)	~P∪~Q∪~R
T	T	T	F	F	F	T	F	F	T	F	F
F	T	T	F	F	T	F	T	F	T	F	T
T	F	T	F	T	F	F	T	F	T	F	T
F	F	T	F	T	T	F	T	F	T	F	T
T	T	F	T	F	F	F	T	F	T	F	T
F	T	F	T	F	T	F	T	F	T	F	T
T	F	F	T	T	F	F	T	F	T	F	T
F	F	F	T	T	T	F	T	T	F	T	T

Make a truth table for each of the following propositional forms.

(P ∩ Q) U ~Q

~ (P ∩ Q)

(P U ~Q) ∩ R

~P ∩ ~Q

P ∩ ~P

If P, Q, and R are true while S and T are false, which of the following are true?

(~P) U (Q ∩ ~Q)

(~P) U (~Q)

[(~Q) U S] ∩ (Q U S)

(S ∩ R) U (S ∩ T)

(P U S) ∩ (P U T)

[(~T ∩ P) U (T ∩ P)

(~P) ∩ (Q U ~Q)

~R ∩ ~S

66

Competition

To qualify for the competition, the applicant must be a female, less than 21 years of age, and Canadian (A ∩ B ∩ C).

Find the appropriate row that reflects each person indicated below. Indicate whether the person can compete.

A	B	C				
Sex Female	Age < 21 years of age	Canadian Citizenship	Female, age 20, U.S.	Female, age 22, Canadian	Male, age 33, Canadian	Male, age 21, U.S.
T	T	T				
F	T	T				
T	F	T				
F	F	T				
T	T	F				
F	T	F				
T	F	F				
F	F	F				

Conditional Statements

Conditional statement = If A, then B

Converse of the conditional statement = If B, then A

The converse of a conditional statement is not necessarily true. The Truth Table for a conditional statement is listed below (Smith et al., 2006). Proposition A is the antecedent and B is the consequence.

A	B	A $\rightarrow$ B
T	T	T
F	T	T
T	F	F
F	F	T

The table above indicates that the conditional statement is true if and only if A is false or B is true.

Suppose you state to your child that if she behaves, then you will give her candy. Let us look at the four possibilities and their associated truth values.

Let **A = child behaves;   B = you give child candy**

A	B	A $\rightarrow$ B
A = False: The child misbehaves	B = True: You give child candy	You are truthful (T), because your guarantee did not address the child's misbehavior
A = False: The child misbehaves	B = False: You do not give child candy	You are truthful (T), because your guarantee did not address the child's misbehavior
A = True: The child behaves	B = True: You give child candy	You are truthful (T), because you honored your guarantee
A = True: The child behaves	B = False: You do not give child candy	You are not truthful (F), because you did not honor your guarantee

Below are conditional statements along with their converse statements.

If the person was aggressive, then the person was arrested.
If the person was arrested, then the person was aggressive.

If you arrested a person, then you seized the person.
If you seized the person, then you arrested the person.

If you interrogated the suspect, then you Mirandized the suspect.
If you Mirandized the suspect, then you interrogated the suspect.

For the conditional statements below, write its converse statement.

If you bought a TV, then you are broke.

If you are the police, then you can arrest.

If you surf, then you are in water.

If I was sad, then I cried.

If you are Catholic, then you are Christian.

<u>Examples to Demonstrate Difference</u>

If you are arrested, then you have been seized. However, if you are seized does not necessarily mean that you have been arrested. If you are sad, then you cry. However, if you cry does not necessarily mean that you are sad.

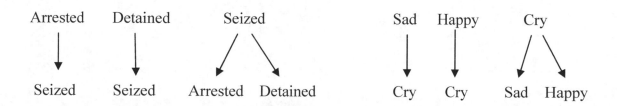

EXAMPLE: LAW H broken down into Levels of Headings

I.

    A.

        1.

            a.   and

            b.   and

            c.;   or

        2.

            a.   or

            b.;   and

        3.;   and

    B.

        1.   and

        2.;   or

    C.

        1.

            a.   or

            b.;   and

        2.;   or

II.

    A.

        1.

            a.   and

            b.;   or

        2.

            a.;   or

            b.   and

            c.;   or

    B.   or

C.

    1.

        a.   and

        b.;   and

    2.;   or

III.

    A.

        1.

            a.   or

            b.;   or

        2.;   or

        3.

            a.   and

            b.;   or

            c.;   and

    B.

        1.   and

        2.;   and

    C.

        1.

            a.   and

            b.;   and

        2.;   and

IV.

The same LAW H and Levels of Headings using ∩ and U

Law = True if   (I.   U   II.   U   III.   ∩   IV.)   = T

           I. = True if   (A. ∩ B. U C.)   = T

               A. = T if (1. U 2. ∩ 3.)   = T

                     1.= true if (a. ∩ b. ∩ c.)   = T
                     2. Is true if (a. U b.)   = T
                     3. = true if 3   = T

               B. = T if (1. ∩ 2)   = T

                     1. = true if 1.   = T
                     2. = true if 2.   = T

              C. = true if (1. ∩ 2.)   = T
                   1.= true if (a. U b.)   = T
                   2.= true if 2   = T

        II. = True if   (A. U B. U C)   = T

              A. = T if (1. U 2.)   = T

                     1. = True if (a. ∩ b.)   = T
                     2. = True if [a. U (b. ∩ c.) = T

              B. = T if B. =   = T

C. = T if (1. ∩ 2)   = T

      1. = True if (a. ∩ b.)   = T
      2. = True if 2   = T

III. = True if (A. ∩ B. ∩ C)   = T

    A. = T if [(1. U 2.) U 3]   = T

      1. = True if (a. U b.)   = T
      2. = True if 2   = T
      3. = True if [(a. ∩ b.) U c.]   = T

    B. = T if (1. ∩ 2.)   = T
     1. = true if 1. =   = T
     2. = true if 2. =   = T

    C. = T if (1. ∩ 2)   = T

      1. = True if (a. ∩ b.)   = T
      2. = True if 2   = T
IV. = True if IV.   = T

Exercise 1

Policy: If you want to park your car at the school, you must:

I.   Request a parking permit in writing and:
       (a_1) Be a student with at least a 3.0 GPA or
       (b_1) Be a family member of a current student at the school; and
       (c_1) Pay \$20; or

II. Be a graduate of the school and:
       (a_2) Be a lifetime member of the school; and
       (b_2) Paid dues in full; and
       (c_2) Display lifetime member sticker in car window.

Use $\cap$ and $\cup$ to write the above in mathematical terms.

Suppose:

I, a_1, c_1, c_2 are all True

II, b_1, a_2, b_2 are all False

Will the person be able to park her car at the school?

Exercise 2

Consider the following statement (elements of the law):

Law = Arrest a person who is intoxicated, has no excuse, and is not on own property, or a person who shoots a gun in public with no excuse

Let

A = person is intoxicated

B = has an excuse

C = Person is on own property

D = person shoots gun

Use the variables provided and use ∩ and U to write the law in mathematical terms.

Evaluate whether you will arrest each of the following suspects if the following conditions exist?

Suspect 1:   A, D = true; B, C = false

Suspect 2:   A, C = false; B, D = true

Exercise 3

Consider the following statement (elements of the law):

Law = Arrest a person who is intoxicated and who shoots a gun, or a person who is not on his own property and shoots a gun with no excuse

Let

A = person is intoxicated

B = has an excuse

C = Person is on own property

D = person shoots gun

Use the variables provided and use ∩ and U to write the law in mathematical terms.

Evaluate whether you will arrest each of the following suspects if the following conditions exist?

Suspect 1:   A, D = true; B, C = false

Suspect 2:   A, C = false; B, D = true

Exercise 4

Consider the following statement (elements of the law):

Law = Arrest a person who is intoxicated and in public, or a person who is intoxicated and shoots a gun

Let

A = person is intoxicated

B = has an excuse

C = Person is on own property

D = person shoots gun

<u>Use the variables provided and use ∩ and U to write the law in mathematical terms.</u>

Evaluate whether you will arrest each of the following suspects if the following conditions exist?

Suspect 1:   A, D = true; B, C = false

Suspect 2:   A, C = false; B, D = true

Exercise 5: Public Disorderly Conduct

Use the public disorderly conduct law, assign variables, and use ∩ and U to write the law in mathematical terms.

References

Smith, S., Eggen, M., St. Andre, R. (2006). *A transition to advanced mathematics* (6th ed.). Belmont, CA: Thomson Brooks/Cole.

CHAPTER 5. BOOLEAN ALGEBRA, BASES, & VENN DIAGRAMS

(Ahmad, 2004; Broudy, 1970; Diaz, 2012; Gillie, 1965; Large, 2006; Purplemath, 2012; Roth, 1979)

This section on Boolean algebra aids in the development of critical thinking skills via flow charts, truth tables, Venn Diagrams, and Boolean Operations. First, flow charting requires a person to follow instructions. It is imperative that law enforcement personnel consistently adhere to procedures and policies by following instructions. Second, although truth tables and Venn Diagrams have different formats, they both use Boolean Operations on variables and combinations of variables to create a designed condition or specific outcome. Third, the process of following instructions can be seen in Boolean Operations via circuit designs, which combine truth table operations with flowcharting. In short, a number of variables, such as the elements of a law, can be evaluated via Boolean Operations.

Laws & Theorems of Boolean Algebra

Idempotent laws: $A \cdot A = A$; $B + B = B$

OPERATION **AND**

A AND B = A ∩ B = A · B = A ∧ B

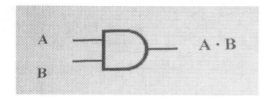

INPUT		OUTPUT (A AND B)
A	B	A ∩ B
T	T	T
F	T	F
T	F	F
F	F	F

OPERATION **OR**

A OR B = A U B = A + B = A V B

INPUT		OUTPUT (A OR B)
A	B	A U B
T	T	T
F	T	T
T	F	T
F	F	F

OPERATION **NOT**

NOT A = ~A = $\overline{A}$ = A′

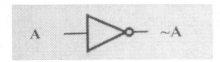

INPUT	OUTPUT (NOT A)
A	~ A
T	F
F	T

OPERATION **NAND** = NOT AND = $\overline{A \cdot B}$ = ~ (A · B) = (A ∩ B)′ = $\overline{(A \cap B)}$

$\overline{(A \cap B)}$

INPUT			OUTPUT
A	B	(A ∩ B)	~ (A ∩ B)
T	T	T	F
F	T	F	T
T	F	F	T
F	F	F	T

80

Involution law: $\sim \overline{(C)} = C$

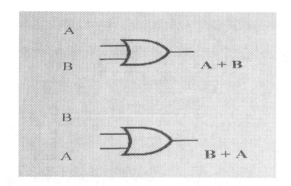

Commutative laws: $A + B = B + A$; $A \cdot B = B \cdot A$

$A + B = B + A$

$A \cdot B = B \cdot A$

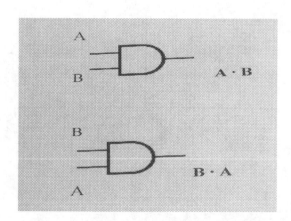

Associative laws: (A + B) + C = A + (B + C);   (A · B) · C = A · (B · C)

(A + B) + C = A + B + C

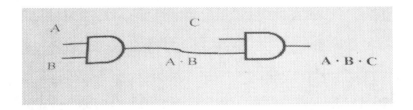

(B + C) + A = A + B + C

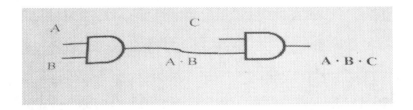

(A · B) · C = A · B · C

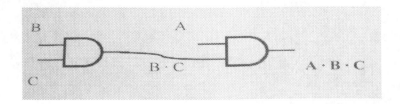

(B · C) · A = A · B · C

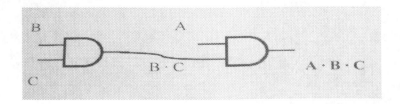

Distributive laws: $A \cdot (B + C) = (A \cdot B) + (A \cdot C);$ $A + (B \cdot C) = (A + B) \cdot (A + C)$

$A \cdot (B + C) = (A \cdot B) + (A \cdot C)$

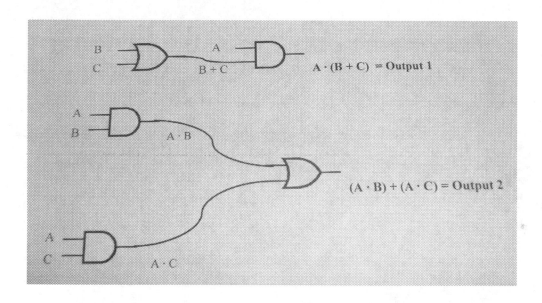

A	B	C	B + C	Output 1 A · (B + C)	(A · B)	(A · C)	Output 2 (A · B) + (A · C)
T	T	T	T	**T**	T	T	**T**
F	T	T	T	**F**	F	F	**F**
T	F	T	T	**T**	F	T	**T**
F	F	T	T	**F**	F	F	**F**
T	T	F	T	**T**	T	F	**T**
F	T	F	T	**F**	F	F	**F**
T	F	F	F	**F**	F	F	**F**
F	F	F	F	**F**	F	F	**F**

$$A + (B \cdot C) = (A + B) \cdot (A + C)$$

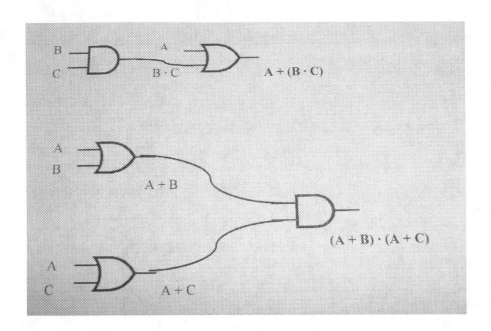

A	B	C	(B · C)	A + (B · C)	(A + B)	(A + C)	(A + B) · (A + C)
T	T	T	T	**T**	T	T	**T**
F	T	T	T	**T**	T	T	**T**
T	F	T	F	**T**	T	T	**T**
F	F	T	F	**F**	F	T	**F**
T	T	F	F	**T**	T	T	**T**
F	T	F	F	**F**	T	F	**F**
T	F	F	F	**T**	T	T	**T**
F	F	F	F	**F**	F	F	**F**

OPERATION **NOR** = NOT OR = ~ OR = (A + B)´ = ~ (A V B) = $\overline{(A \cup B)}$ = $\overline{A + B}$

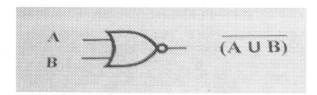

INPUT			OUTPUT
A	B	(A ∪ B)	~ (A ∪ B)
1	1	1	0
0	1	1	0
1	0	1	0
0	0	0	1

OPERATION **EXCLUSIVE OR = XOR = (A + B) BUT NOT (A ∩ B)**

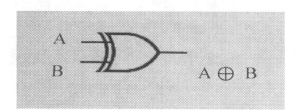

INPUT		OUTPUT
A	B	A ⊕ B
1	1	0
0	1	1
1	0	1
0	0	0

OPERATION **XNOR = ~ [(A + B) BUT NOT (A ∩ B)]**

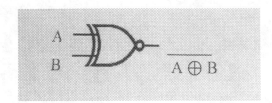

INPUT			OUTPUT
A	B	$A \oplus B$	$\overline{A \oplus B}$
1	1	0	1
0	1	1	0
1	0	1	0
0	0	0	1

Equivalence operation ≡

When X has the same value as Y

X	Y	$X \equiv Y$
T	T	T
F	T	F
T	F	F
F	F	T

Conditional Statement A → B

If A, then B

A	B	A → B
T	T	T
F	T	T
T	F	F
F	F	T

The table above indicates that the conditional statement is true if and only if A is false or B is true.

Below are different bases for numeric communication (Roth, 1979).

Decimal (base 10) $(10^4)(10^3)(10^2)(10^1)(10^0)$	Binary (base 2) $(2^4)(2^3)(2^2)(2^1)(2^0)$	Octal (base 8) $(8^4)(8^3)(8^2)(8^1)(8^0)$	Hexadecimal (base 16) $(16^4)(16^3)(16^2)(16^1)(16^0)$
0	0	0	0
1	1	1	1
2	10	2	2
3	11	3	3
4	100	4	4
5	101	5	5
6	110	6	6
7	111	7	7
8	1000	10	8
9	1001	11	9
10	1010	12	A
11	1011	13	B
12	1100	14	C
13	1101	15	D
14	1110	16	F
15	1111	17	F
16	10000	20	10
20	10100	24	14
40	101000	50	28
200	11001000	310	C8

Example: Write the value of 200 in decimal.

Then write its equivalent value in binary, octal, and hexadecimal.

Show your work.

$$200_{10} = 2(10^2) + 0(10^1) + 0(10^0)$$

$$11001000_2 = 1(2^7) + 1(2^6) + 0(2^5) + 0(2^4) + 1(2^3) + 0(2^2) + 0(2^1) + 0(2^0)$$

$$310_8 = 3(8^2) + 1(8^1) + 0(8^0) = 200$$

$$C8_{16} = C(16^1) + 8(16^0)$$

Problems

    1. Convert to octal and binary

a. 333_{10} b. 76_{16} c. 812_{10}

    2. Convert to hexadecimal

a. 174_2 b. 4523_8 c. 777_{10}

    3. Convert to decimal

a. 87_4 b. 452_3 c. 627_5

Below are different codes for numeric communication (Roth, 1979).

Decimal digit	8-4-2-1 code	6-3-1-1 code
0	0000	0000
1	0001	0001
2	0010	0011
3	0011	0100
4	0100	0101
5	0101	0111
6	0110	1000
7	0111	1001
8	1000	1011
9	1001	1100

Examples

$N = 7_{10} = 0111$ [8-4-2-1 code] $= 0(8) + 1(4) + 1(2) + 1(1)$

$N = 7_{10} = 1001$ [6-3-1-1 code] $= 1(6) + 0(3) + 0(1) + 1(1)$

$N = 77_{10} = 0111\ 0111$ [8-4-2-1 code]

$N = 77_{10} = 1001\ 1001$ [6-3-1-1 code]

VENN DIAGRAMS

(Gillie, 1965; Large, 2006; Purplemath, 2012)

The universe establishes the entire set of parameters being considered. In other words, the universe sets the boundaries for consideration. Some of the variables within the universe may interact and overlap with one another. The Venn diagram represents the variables within the universe and their interactions.

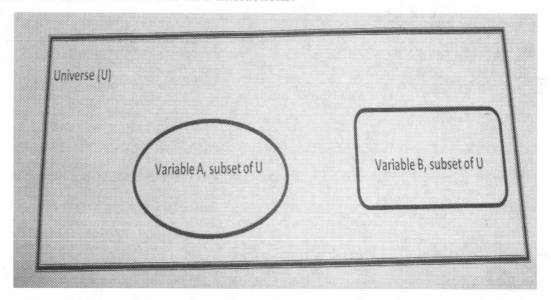

Example: Universe = deck of playing cards, without jokers

A = face cards
B= even cards

Q1: How many cards are there for variable A and for variable B?

Q2: Where will the jokers fit on the above figure?

The colored circles below represent the label above the diagram.

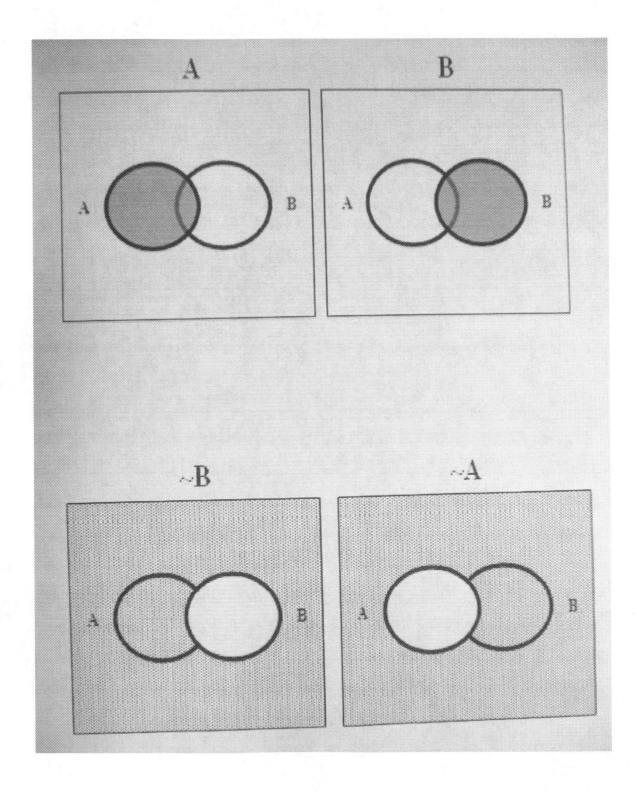

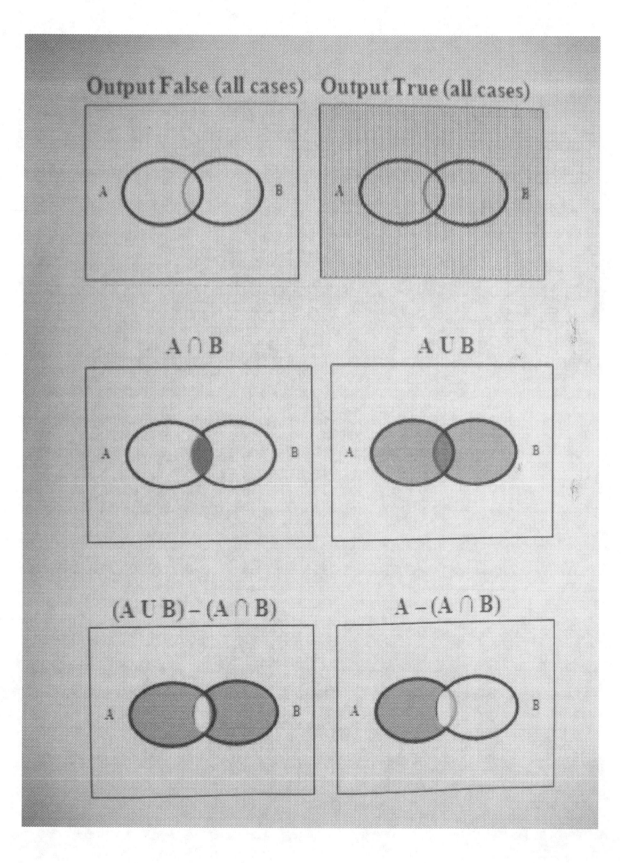

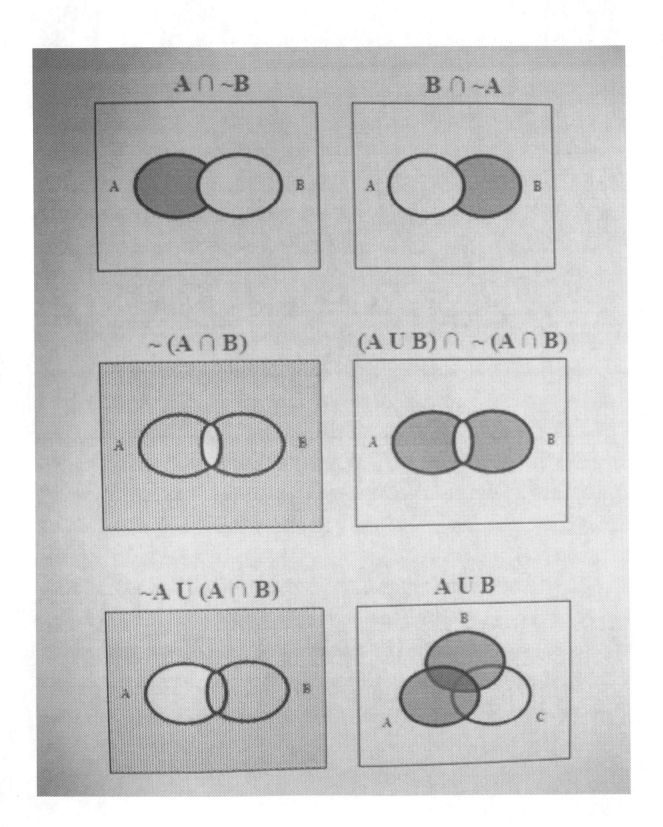

A ∩ B ∩ C

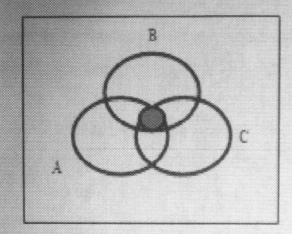

~(A ∩ B ∩ C)

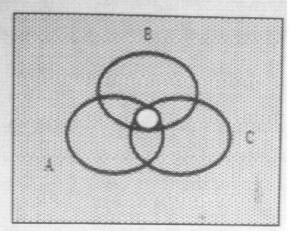

~A ∩ ~B ∩ ~C

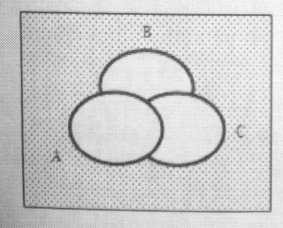

~A U ~B U ~C

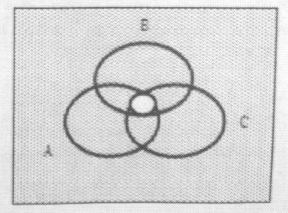

Venn Diagrams can be used to see how different variables interact. The universe is designated by the rectangular boundary. In other words, everything inside of the rectangle represents the population. The circles represent particular variables that are contained within the universe. With three variables, there are 2^3 different combinations of variables. In other words, with three variables there are 8 different possibilities, which are represented by the 8 different colors in *Figure 4*. The 8 different colors in *Figure 4* are red, blue, yellow, orange, green, purple, black, and white (the part of the universe that is not inside any of the circles). It is important to note that Male/Female is only one variable. If a circle represents males, then everything outside of the circle would represent females. See *Table 2* for the interpretation of *Figure 4*.

Table 2
Interpretation of Figure 4 Venn Diagram

Color	Representation		
Red	Male	< 21 years of age	Not blond hair
Blue	Female	< 21 years of age	Blond hair
Yellow	Female	≥ 21 years of age	Not blond hair
Orange	Male	≥ 21 years of age	Not blond hair
Green	Female	≥ 21 years of age	Blond hair
Purple	Male	< 21 years of age	Blond hair
Black	Male	≥ 21 years of age	Blond hair
White	Female	< 21 years of age	Not blond hair

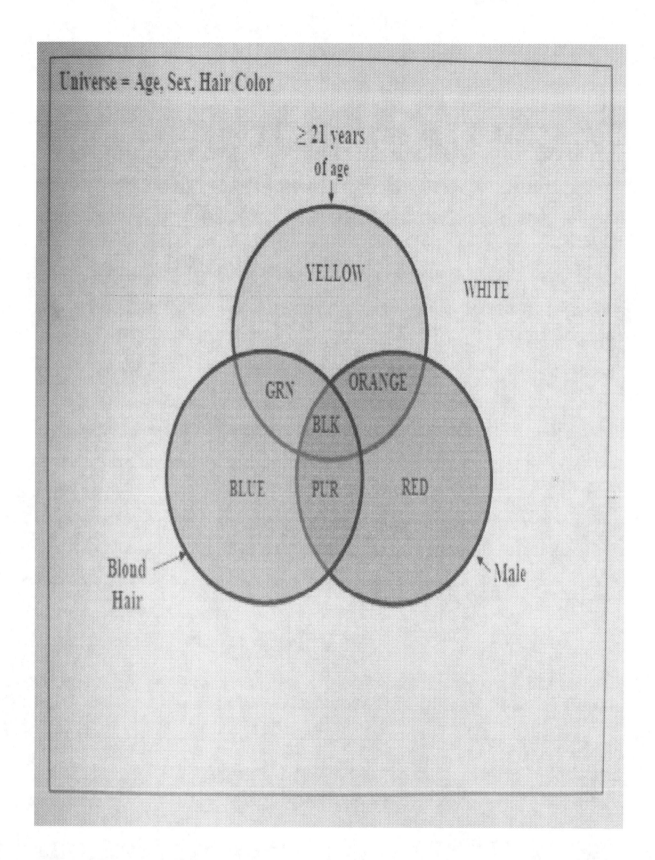

Figure 4. Venn Diagram.

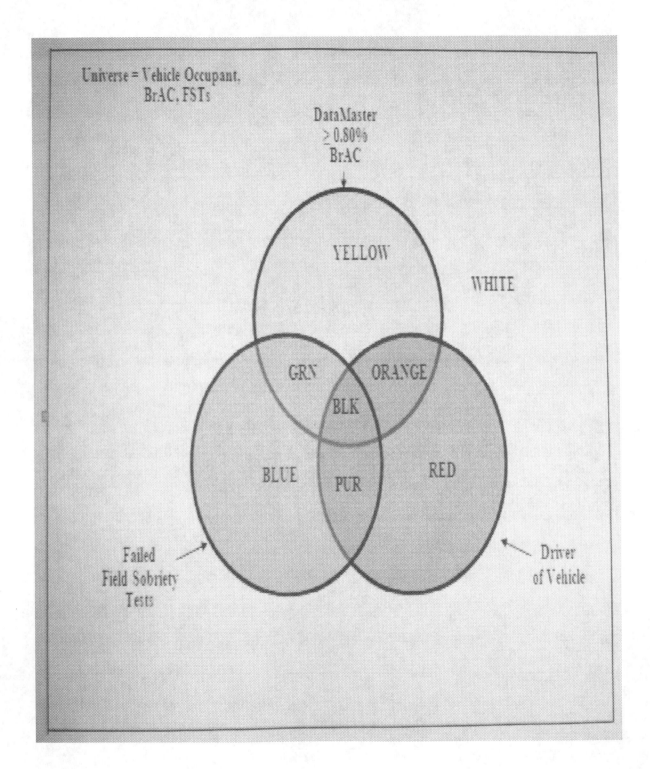

Figure 5. DUI Venn Diagram.

Complete the table below based on *Figure 5*.   BrAC = Breath Alcohol Concentration; FSTs = Field Sobriety Tests. Indicate proper status for each box.

Color	Driver (Yes/No)	BrAC $\geq$ 0.80% (Yes/No)	FSTs (Pass/Failed)
Red			
Blue			
Yellow			
Orange			
Green			
Purple			
Black			
White			

Using *Figure 5*, indicate the color the matches the description.

Description	Color
Driver, DataMaster = 2.2 BrAC, passed Field Sobriety Tests	
Driver, DataMaster = 0.7 BrAC, passed Field Sobriety Tests	
Driver, DataMaster = 0.7 BrAC, failed Field Sobriety Tests	
Driver, DataMaster = 1.1 BrAC, failed Field Sobriety Tests	
Passenger, DataMaster = 1.9 BrAC, passed Field Sobriety Tests	
Passenger, DataMaster = 0.4 BrAC, passed Field Sobriety Tests	
Passenger, DataMaster = 0.0 BrAC, failed Field Sobriety Tests	
Passenger, DataMaster = 1.5 BrAC, failed Field Sobriety Tests	

Venn Diagram Exercises

Draw Venn Diagrams for the following three scenarios.   Define the three variables (age, sex, race) and use circles to represent the variables. Use the same three variables for each of the three diagrams. In other words, once the universe and circles are drawn, use the exact same universe and circles for each of the diagrams.

1) Of all South Carolina residents, people from 21-50 years of age, white, female

2) Of all South Carolina residents, people from 21-50 years of age, black, male

3) Of all South Carolina residents, people not 21-50 years of age, black, female

Create a Venn Diagram to represent each equation in column Q and column R. Represent the equations by shading in the Venn Diagrams. For each of the 5 scenarios, compare the Venn Diagram of column Q to column R and state which equation covers more area. Let a law violation be represented by column Q and the suspect's actions be represented by column R. For each of the following 5 scenarios, indicate whether an arrest will be made. An arrest will be made if R is a subset of Q.

	Q	R	Larger Area (Q or R)	Arrest (Y or N)
1)	$\sim A \cap \sim B$	$\sim (A \cap B)$		
2)	$\sim A \cup \sim B$	$\sim (A \cup B)$		
3)	$A \cap B$	$A \cup B$		
4)	$A \cup \sim B$	$A \cap \sim B$		
5)	$\sim (A \cup B) \cap C$	$(\sim A \cup \sim B) \cup C$		

VENN DIAGRAM

For the following four questions, use only 2 circles labeled A and B in the Universe. The intersecting area of A and B = C.

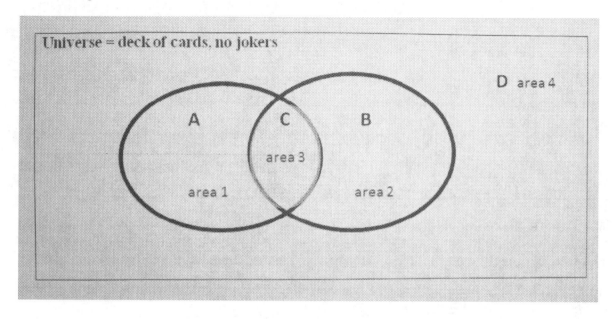

A - C = area 1

B - C = area 2

C = area 3

D = area 4 (items that are not contained in areas 1, 2, or 3)

Question 1: Use a regular deck of playing cards (no jokers).

A = RED CARDS

B = FACE CARDS

1) How many cards are in area 1?

2) How many cards are in area 2?

3) How many cards are in area 3?

4) How many cards are in area 4?

Question 2: Use a regular deck of playing cards (no jokers).

A = RED CARDS

B = BLACK CARDS

5) How many cards are in area 1?

6) How many cards are in area 2?

7) How many cards are in area 3?

8) How many cards are in area 4?

Question 3: Use a regular deck of playing cards (no jokers).

A = DIAMONDS

B = EVEN CARDS (NO FACE CARDS)

9) How many cards are in area 1?

10) How many cards are in area 2?

11) How many cards are in area 3?

12) How many cards are in area 4?

Question 4: Use a regular deck of playing cards (no jokers).

A = HEARTS

B = JACKS

13) How many cards are in area 1?

14) How many cards are in area 2?

15) How many cards are in area 3?

16) How many cards are in area 4?

References

Ahmad, M (2004). *Boolean algebra.* Retrieved from http://imps.mcmaster.ca/courses/ CAS-701-04/presentations/contributions/Ahmadi-boolean-alg.pdf

Broudy, R.L. (1970). *Modern math made easy.* Irvington-on-Hudson, NY: Harvey House.

Diaz, M.O. (2012). *Boolean algebra & logic gates.* Retrieved from http://www.scribd.com/ doc/ 59329027/30/XNOR

Gillie, A.C. (1965). *Binary arithmetic and Boolean algebra.* New York, NY: McGraw-Hill.

Large, L. (2006). *Illustrated dictionary of math.* Saffron Hill, London: Usborne.

Purplemath (2012). *Venn Diagrams & Set Notation. Retrieved from* http://www.purple math.com/modules/venndiag2.htm

Roth, C.H. (1979). *Fundamental of logic design* (2nd ed.). St. Paul, MN: West.

CHAPTER 6. ENGLISH, LOGIC, & QUANTIFIERS

Quantitative v. Qualitative Studies

Quantitative investigations are scientific, objective, and effective in describing phenomena in terms of magnitude (Balian, 1988). Quantitative investigations use numeric values and statistics to identify patterns, to objectively quantify relationships between variables, and to make predictions. In addition, because larger sample sizes are used, data can be generalized to larger populations. However, numeric values are ineffective in describing the subjective interpretations of human emotions (Wakefield, 1995). Because individuals have unique lived experiences and their realities are based on their own perceptions, a single objective truth is unattainable; indeed, there are multiple realities when dealing with perceptions. Thus, quantitative investigations are ineffective for the reconstruction of meanings. In short, quantitative studies ask how variables are related but not why they are related. For example, a quantitative research question may ask, *Is there a relationship between ice cream sales and the murder rate?* By the way, there is a positive relationship.

When investigating a topic which cannot be quantitatively predicted, such as human nature, qualitative investigations are most effective. Indeed, qualitative investigations are preferred for describing and interpreting experiences in context specific settings because each person's reality is construed in his or her own mind; qualitative research attempts to reveal the meanings that participants have given to various phenomena (Adams, 1999; Ponterotto, 2005). This kind of information cannot be attained through quantitative analysis and requires probing the participants for greater detail through in-depth interviews using open ended questions. In short, qualitative studies ask why variables are related but not how they are related. For example, a qualitative research question may ask, *Why do you feel that ice cream sales are related to the murder rate?*

Falsification

Theories are an organized body of principles and concepts intended to explain specific phenomena (Leedy & Ormrod, 2005). A police officer can test a theory to determine if it is a viable explanation of a phenomenon by developing and statistically verifying a conjecture concerning the relationship between the variables. However, because human knowledge is limited, hypotheses cannot actually be proved true (Shields, 2007). For example, we will never know for sure if any of the many extraneous variables have impacted a particular relationship between known variables (a person may appear to have committed a crime, but appearances can be deceiving). However, we can demonstrate that relationships do not exist between variables (the person was already dead at the time of the crime and could not have committed the crime). Thus, because relationships cannot be proved true, an attempt is made to prove them false. This is called falsification. For example, instead of proving that a defendant is truly guilty of a crime, a prosecutor attempts to prove with a certain confidence level that the defendant is not innocent of the crime. For example, if there is a 95% confidence level that a defendant is not innocent, then jurors may find the defendant guilty. In other words, if hypotheses are not proved false, then they are accepted as true at a certain confidence level. This implies that there is an acceptable level of being wrong. Thus, innocent people may sometimes be wrongly convicted.

For a trial verdict, there are two possible ways to make a mistake. One way is to convict an innocent person. The other way is to set a guilty person free. A juror can ensure that one type of error is never made, but this will require either a) always setting defendants free or b) always convicting defendants. For either case, there is no need for a trial. On the one hand, if one juror wants to ensure that he never makes a mistake by letting a guilty person go free, then that juror must always vote guilty. His reasoning may be that the police do not arrest innocent persons. With this reasoning, there is no need for a trial because everyone arrested will be convicted by this type of juror. On the other hand, if another juror wants to ensure that she never makes a mistake by sending an innocent person to jail, then that juror must always vote not guilty. With this reasoning, there is no need for a trial because everyone arrested will be set free by this type of juror. Thus, in both cases, there is no need for a trial. However, there are trials in the U.S., which means that there is compromise and the chance of making mistakes.

Negotiations are required among jury members. If a mistake is made, then the question is whether U.S. jurors want to error on the side of convicting innocent individuals or to error on the side of setting guilty individuals free. By design, the U.S. legal system is set up to error on the side of letting guilty persons go free. A conviction is based on guilt beyond a reasonable doubt; an acquittal is not based on innocence beyond a reasonable doubt. As indicated in *Figure 6*, because decisions are based on confidence levels and negotiations, innocent individuals will sometimes be convicted. This is an inherent part of the U.S. legal system. Notice that this argument is not influenced by the penalty of the conviction, such as the death penalty. In other words, it is expected that innocent persons will sometimes be convicted and be put to death.

<u>Levels of Proof</u>

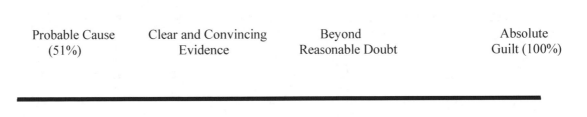

Figure 6. Acceptable Chance of Wrongful Conviction. (not to scale)

Assumptions

Most decisions depend on assumptions, and we will never know if all of the assumptions are 100% accurate. Although we may be confident about a decision, we cannot know with absolute certainty that the decision is correct. However, understanding the assumptions that were relied upon in making a decision is important because the assumptions may change, which may impact an objective decision. In law enforcement, if the assumptions change, then police officers must be willing to modify their position.

Correlation does not mean causation (Leedy & Ormrod, 2005). Just because two events are highly correlated does not mean that one event causes the other. For example, it does not get dark at night because the sun is on the other side of the earth (Verma, 2005). The sun is an additional light source, but it is not the only light source in the sky. Thus, in this case, a wrong assumption may lead one to believe that the lack of sunlight causes it to get dark at night.

Being not false is not the same thing as being true. In order words, if something is not negative, this does not mean that it is positive (i.e., it may be neutral). For example, if a basketball team has played 10 games and is undefeated, what is the team's record? It is unknown because the team may have tied any number of the 10 games. If by some chance the team had tied all 10 games, a defense attorney may claim that the team has never lost, while the prosecutor may claim that the team has never won. Both statements are true, yet they seem to be contradictory. However, the two statements do not necessarily conflict with one another. This is how statistics can be misleading. Should consumers buy the same shoes used by the team? Either decision may be argued and supported with statistical data.

Police officers need to detect diversionary flares (i.e., deception) that are intended to lead the officer off track. The way to do this is to get the sought after answers to their questions via active voice questions and answers. For example, if an individual answers questions through double negatives or through misplaced modifiers, the officer must clarify the answers by asking direct questions that elicit active voice responses. See *Table 3*.

Table 3
Interpretation of Sport Statement

	Interpretation of Results		
	Won (+)	Tied (neutral)	Lost (-)
Suspect statement			
I have not lost	X	X	
I have not won		X	X
I have won	X		
I have lost			X

It should be pointed out in Table 3 that "I have won ≠ I have not lost". For a second example, suppose we state that the sky was not cloudy all day. All day means 100% of the time. Therefore, we are stating that it was not cloudy 100% of the time; it could have been cloudy 0% of the time up to 99% of the time. In other words, it could have been sunny 1% of the time up to 100% of the time. If we are writing a police report and it is important that the sky was sunny during the crime, stating that the sky was not cloudy all day may be detrimental to our case. See *Table 4*.

Table 4

Interpretation of Weather Statement

	Interpretation of Statement		
	Sunny all day	Cloudy up to 99% of time	Cloudy all day (100% of time)
Not cloudy all day	X	X	

Now suppose that a police officer arrives at a crash scene. A car that was parked near a curb pulled out into traffic and was struck by another car headed in the same direction. If the police officer asks a witness to the crash what she saw, and if she states that she did not see the driver in the parked car look before he pulled out into traffic, the officer must evaluate the value of the statement of the witness. See *Table 5*.

108

Table 5
Interpretation of Witness Statement

	Interpretation of Witness Statement		
	I saw driver look	I was not looking	I saw driver not look
Witness statement provided		X	X
Answer sought (two good responses)	X		X

Thus, the witness statement provided has little value. Notice the first four words: "I did not see." This is problematic because the police officer wants to know what the witness did see. Indeed, the witness statement never claimed that the driver of the parked car did not look before he pulled out into traffic. The witness statement would be true even if the witness was not looking in the right direction at the time of the crash. It would be wrong to assume that the witness was looking in the right direction. To argue in court that the witness saw the driver of the parked car not look would be changing the truth value of the witness statement. In short, a police officer needs to be careful about relying on assumptions. Get responses that provide direct and positive answers.

Also, police officers must not assume that all individuals define words in the same way. For example, consider the following statements.

Unclear: Where were you during dinner?
Clear: Where were you during supper?

The above sentence that mentions dinner is problematic because dinner is not time dependent. Although supper is the last meal of the day, dinner is the largest meal of the day. Thus, for some people, dinner may not be the same as supper. In other words, if you were to question a suspect about his or her alibi during dinner time, you may be thinking about

109

5:00 pm and the individual may be speaking about noon. Therefore, seek precise times of day that do not have different meanings to different individuals.

Misplaced and dangling modifiers

Grammar is important in police writing because an officer's credibility is linked to his or her written reports. If police officers make mistakes in their reports, the officers should expect defense attorneys to ask them if they have performed their jobs to the best of their ability. On the one hand, if the officers claim that they have done their best work, then mistakes in their reports will make them appear incompetent or dishonest. On the other hand, if the officers claim that they have not done their best work, then mistakes in their reports will make them appear lazy and uncaring. Thus, police officers need to use proper grammar when writing police reports.

Although some mistakes in grammar may make police officers look incompetent, lazy, or dishonest in court, other mistakes in grammar may significantly change the meaning of a police report. For example, because a misplaced modifier incorrectly modifies the wrong word, and because a dangling modifier has no referent in a sentence, misplaced and dangling modifiers may alter the meaning of a sentence. Thus, adjectives and adverbs should be placed as closely as possible to the words that they are supposed to modify and active voice should be employed (American Psychological Association, 2010). This may help eliminate any unintended meanings. In this case, the police officers should expect defense attorneys to ask them if they write true and accurate reports. If the officers state that their reports are true and accurate, then the defense attorney may argue that the reports should be accepted at face value, especially if misplaced modifiers change the meaning of the police reports to mean what the defense attorneys want them to mean. However, if the officers state that their reports are not true and accurate, then the reports will have little value, the officers' credibility will be ruined, and the officers could be criminally charged with filing false police reports.

Consider the following example. Suppose a man and his wife are at school and he tells her that he loves her.

Incorrect statement: He told his wife that he loves her at the school.

Correct statement: While at the school, he told his wife that he loves her.

The incorrect statement does not indicate that he loves his wife, but it does indicate that he loves his wife's presence at the school. This would be appropriate, for example, if his wife worked at a school and he did not want her to quit her job and to leave the school.

Incorrect statement: Running out of gas, she walked to the gas station.

Correct statement: She walked to the gas station because her car ran out of gas.

The incorrect sentence indicates that she ran out of gas (not her car). This may imply that she was jogging, became tired, and started to walk.

Logic: Conditional Statements

Although an if-then statement may be true, the converse of an if-then statement may not necessarily be true (Smith, Eggen, & St. Andre, 2006). In other words, the converse of a conditional statement is not necessarily true. For example, research shows that aggressive behaviors in children are good predictors of adult criminality (Huesmann & Eron, 1992; Huesmann et al., 2002; Miller-Johnson et al., 2005). Thus, if aggression is present then there is crime. However, if crime is present does not necessarily mean that there is aggression (e.g., there may be other reasons why people are arrested).

Repeating an earlier example, suppose a father states to his daughter that if she behaves, then he will give her candy. Then suppose his daughter misbehaves. The only guarantee that the father made was that he will act in a certain way if his daughter behaves. However, the father never addressed what he will do if his daughter misbehaves. Thus, if his daughter misbehaves, the father's actions will be truthful whether or not his gives his

111

daughter candy. The father will only be untruthful if his daughter behaves and the father does not give her candy. See *Table 6*.

Table 6
Interpretation of Statement

Guarantee		If my daughter behaves...	If my daughter misbehaves...
If my daughter behaviors, then I will give her candy		Then a truthful statement dictates that I give her candy	Then a truthful statement allows me to either give her candy or to not give her candy

Let us apply this argument to a law. A U.S. visa is an entry document issued by the U.S. government that allows a non-citizen to seek entry into the U.S. (LexisNexis, 2005). A non-American passport is issued by the person's native country and is a travel document that is used for identification and proof of citizenship. **Suppose federal law states that a particular person cannot enter the U.S. without a passport.** Thus, if the person has entered the U.S., then the person must have had a passport (this is a true statement). However, it is not necessarily true that if the person has a passport, then the person will be allowed to enter the U.S. The law states that not having a passport will prevent the person's entry into the U.S., but the law does not address what will happen if the person does have a passport. See *Table 7*. Thus, understanding the converse of conditional statements is important in law enforcement.

Table 7
Interpretation of Law

	Passport Law	
	If have, then may enter	If do not have, then may not enter
Foreign Passport		x

Quantifiers

Because conditional statements can be objectively assessed by turning them into mathematic equations, police officers need to understand the difference between existential and universal quantifiers. It is important for a police officer not to change the meaning of a statement by changing an existential-quantifier statement into a universal-quantifier statement and vice versa. For an open sentence that uses an existential quantifier, the sentence is true if the truth set is nonempty (Smith, Eggen, & St. Andre, 2006). This means that a statement is true if the statement is true at least one time. However, for an open sentence that uses a universal quantifier, the sentence is true only if the truth set is the entire universe. This means that a statement is true only if the statement is true all of the time. For example, if a suspect stated that he likes beer, this statement is true if the suspect likes at least one type of beer. Thus, for the suspect to be lying, an officer will have to prove that the suspect dislikes all types of beer. However, if the suspect stated that he likes all beer, then the officer only needs to show that the suspect dislikes one type of beer for the suspect to be considered untruthful.

Suppose that the signs on a roadway indicate that speed is controlled via RADAR. Then suppose you receive a speeding ticket but the officer used VASCAR to clock your speed. Your argument is that the ticket is invalid because the officer used VASCAR and the signs indicate that RADAR will be used. **What will you have to do in court to show that the signs are not truthful and what does the officer have to do to show that the signs are truthful?** The signs are truthful if at least one officer in the area uses RADAR. Thus, the officer only has to show that one officer in the area uses RADAR. You, on the other hand, will have to show that every officer in the area does not use RADAR.

Subsets

A set is a group of objects that follow a rule or that have something in common (Large, 2006). A subset is a set that belongs to a larger set. Suppose a friend states to you on January 1 that you may borrow his car any day of the year, whenever you want. Then suppose you borrow the car on July 7 and get pulled over by the police. The police charge

113

you with driving another person's car without permission. The police ask you, "Did you have permission to drive the car specifically on July 7?" The police want a *yes* or *no* answer. The correct answer is yes, because July 7 is a part of the year. In other words, the year includes July 7 and you had permission to drive the car on every day of the year.

Suppose John has $20. True or false, John has $10. The answer is true because $10 is a subset of $20. If John has $20, then John has $10.

Consequence of Wrong Assumptions

Magic shows are successful because they challenge the viewers' assumptions. The viewers are led to believe that something is true when it is not true. The next time that you watch a magic trick, try to determine what assumptions you are making.

Assumptions are important because a solution that is based on the wrong assumptions may be ineffective. For example, the effectiveness of the sex offender community notification process relies on the assumptions of the labeling and deterrence theories. Authorities rely on labeling and deterrence in order to get sex predators to **rationally** decide not to commit additional sex crimes due to the high cost. First, people learn to identify other individuals in the way that they are labeled (Vold, Bernard, & Snipes, 2002). Thus, the labeling theory indicates that sex offenders will be easily recognized by local community members if sex offenders are publically labeled and if their crimes are advertised. In regards to Megan's law, it is assumed that all sex offenders are alike and, consequently, they are all labeled as a homogenous group of sex predators (Corrigan, 2006). However, different types of sex offenders are not all motivated by the same reasons. Hence, a single program designed to modify their various behaviors will not work. Second, Megan's law relies on the idea that most sex offenders are strangers to their victims and that offenders are **mentally disturbed** predators who attack without warning or reason. In other words, mentally disturbed predators are expected to make rational decisions. In addition, most sex crimes against children are committed by friends or family members and not by

114

strangers. Thus, community notification efforts are ineffective because they are not in alignment with the problem. Because the research findings do not support the argument that community notification deters stigmatized sex offenders from committing repeat sex offenses, then perhaps programs that rely on theories that support the argument that sex offenders are mentally disturbed need to be investigated (Langevin et. al, 2004; Zevitz, 2006). In other words, limited resources may be better spent on programs that address mental illnesses instead of labeling and rational choice. As stated earlier, the solution to the problem must be in alignment with the theory used to explain the crime. See *Table 8* for various criminal theories and their limitations.

Table 8

Various Theories and their Limitations (Fay, 1987; Schmalleger, 2011; Sower, & Gist, 1994; Sower, Holland, Tiedke, & Freeman, 1957; Turvey & Petherick, 2009)

Theory	Description	Critique
Rational Choice Theory / Deterrence Theory	People freely choose their behaviors. Individuals evaluate the benefits versus costs ratio for each potential course of action. If the benefits are greater than costs, then the decision to perform that act is favorable. Rational choice emphasizes the benefits and deterrence theory emphasizes the costs. Deterrence Theory relies on three factors: Celerity, Severity, & Certainty of Punishment	Overemphasizes importance of individual choice; social factors, such as poverty, are dismissed; does not adequately consider emotions; target hardening causes displacement of crime; factors of deterrence may promote crime if all three factors are not effectively implemented simultaneously (certain, severe, and swift punishment)
Routine Activities Theory	Crime occurs when three elements converge: motivated offenders, attractive targets, and the absence of capable guardians.	Level of motivation is not well defined; because attractive targets and the absence of capable guardians are emphasized more than the motivated offender, identifying and measuring the motivation of offenders is avoided.

Neoclassical Theory	Being tough on crime and retribution will curtail future crime.	Does not explain why crime decreases in areas without tough on crime policies; crime rate reductions may be due to demographic changes in the population.
Biological Theory	First, human beings are biological creatures who are born with certain hardware, such as a brain that controls thought and behavioral development. Because the brain uses a complex chemical-electrical process during the processing of information, any impairment in this process may interfere with the effective operation of the brain. Body shape, diet, hormones, environmental pollution, and chemical factors cause crime.	Denies role of free will; not everyone who is exposed to the same chemicals behave in the same way; why is there no specific diet to cure crime? Increased exposure to pollution and chemicals has not increased the crime rate; cannot explain crime in different parts of the country.
Age-graded Theory	There is a positive relationship between social capital and pro-social behaviors; positive relations are developed over time and lead to pro-social behaviors and reduced crime.	Positive relationships are subjective; some positive relations may provide greater opportunity to commit crime; does not explain why social capital does not prevent everyone from committing crime.
Sociobiology Theory	Behaviors are embedded in the process of natural selection and human survival; crime is the result of territorial struggles.	Fails to consider culture, social learning, and personal experiences; equates humans to animals.
Psychoanalytic Perspective Theory	Crime is the result of poorly developed superegos.	Lacks scientific support; elements of theory were not applied to a wide context for society as a whole.
Modeling Theory	Individuals learn behaviors by observing others who are in the vicinity; individuals are rewarded for aggressive behaviors.	Lacks comprehensive explanatory power.
Behavior Theory	The surrounding environment impacts behavior.	Dismisses cognition in human behavior; punishments may not deter martyrs; some groups believe that punishments are status-enhancing.

Self-control Theory	Individuals have low self-esteem and seek immediate gratification; individuals have little patience and are frustrated easily, which lead to conflict.	Dismisses external factors during different stages of life; oversimplifies the causes of crime.
Ecological Theory	Crime associated with urban transition zones; crime is higher in low income zones near city.	Too much credence to spatial location; does not explain crime outside of socially disorganized areas; correlation does not mean causation.
Strain Theory	Crime is the result of frustration due to blocked opportunities, which prevent success.	The U.S. provides opportunities for all Americans to financially succeed; delinquent juveniles do not report being more stressed than law abiding juveniles; claims that wealth is the single most important goal in life; does not adequately explain the lack of crime for women, who may be stressed as a result of continual discrimination.
Cultural Conflict Theory	Those individuals in power pass laws to protect their own interests.	Can be tautological and may lack explanatory power; may be racist because minorities (who have little power) are labeled as criminals.
Differential Association Theory	Criminal behaviors are learned through communications with intimate others; definitions favorable to crime exceed definitions unfavorable to crime; frequency, duration, intensity, and importance impact the learning of behavior.	Does not sufficiently explain crime; does not consider free choice; does not explain why those surrounded by crime do not commit crime; only accounts for the communication of criminal values, not the emergence of criminal values.
Containment Theory	Crime results when internal (e.g., positive self-esteem) and external (e.g., social groups) control mechanisms fail to protect the individual; like an illness in which only some people who are exposed to social pressures commit crime.	May be feelings of the moment that have been conditioned through individual thought mechanisms.

Social Bond Theory	Weaken bonds between an individual and the social group results in crime; crime is reduced if a person has a strong bond with society, has strong attachments, is committed, and is involved.	Individuals commit crime even when they know that it is wrong; social bonds do not appear strong enough to negate criminal behavior.
Social Control Theory	Delinquent behavior occurs when social constraints on antisocial behaviors are weakened; Control ratio predicts criminal behavior; Control ratio = amount of control personally experienced versus amount of control exercised over others; Too much or too little self-control are equally dangerous.	Assumes that all individuals are automatically deviant unless socialized through control mechanisms; dismisses learned behavior and human motivations.
Labeling Theory	If individuals are arrested, they may become labeled. This may result in a negative stigma being attached to them. This may consequently disrupt their personal relationships and may block their future legitimate economic opportunities, which may lead to more crime.	Does not explain the origin of crime; does not explain secret deviants.
Broken Window Theory	Broken windows, graffiti, litter, abandoned vehicles, homeless persons, and public drinking indicates disorder and a lack of caring. If people do not care about what happens in their neighborhood, then this attracts crime.	May be artifact of police decision-making practices; may bear little objective relationship to the actual degree of crime in area; police may focus more efforts in poor areas and this may mislead media. For example, if the department patrols a certain area with more officers, police will make more arrests in that area (Do more arrests mean safer streets or a more dangerous area?).

Life Course Theory	Human lives are embedded in social relationships across the life span; the impact of various experiences depend on when they occur in life; each person makes choices, which impact each person's life course; a life course is shaped by historic times and places.	Many important life course determinants are experienced during childhood, which means adults may not be accountable for their crimes; individuals may select components of their life course and may influence their own trajectories.
Interactional Theory	Crime is the result of a weakened bond between an individual and society combined with the learning of anti-social behaviors that are rewarded.	Does not fully appreciate childhood maltreatment as an important factor, which leads to crime.
Social Conflict Theory	People in power pass laws to protect their own interests. There is a struggle for power and laws are passed that penalize the disadvantaged.	Overstresses social change and dismisses other well-developed theories of crime; fails to recognize that most people believe crime should be controlled.
Normative Sponsorship Theory	Indicates that people who have a convergence of interest may cooperate with one another in order to satisfy their needs.	Community members will only work together as long as the goals are within the normal limits of established standards.
Dual Taxonomic Theory	Most antisocial children do not become criminals; there are two types of offenders: life course persistent offenders (due to family dysfunction, poverty, neurophysiological deficits, failure in school) and adolescence limited offenders (due to structural disadvantages).	Family and psychological dysfunction are not shown to be directly correlated to parent control or individual trajectories.
Postmodern Criminology	Skeptical of science and scientific method; crime is an integral part of society.	Challenges other theories of crime prevention and control, but fails to offer feasible alternatives.
Convict Criminology	Prisons are too big, hold too many people, and do not reduce crime; to control crime upon release from prison, prisons should focus more on treatment and less on security; based on the lived experiences of convicted felons and ex-inmates.	Most of the authors of the theory are white males, but not all are ex-convicts; authors are biased with agendas; non-convict feminists have been adding to the field, moving the theory from its roots.

Victim Precipitation	Victim unconsciously exhibits behaviors or characteristics that instigate or encourage the attacker; explains multiple victimizations.	Relevant only to violent crime or to particular forms of unlawful violence; assumes that victims and offenders interact prior to crime occurring.
Critical Social Theory	Practical social science that encourages individuals to become socially and politically active in order to change and improve their current social conditions; endorses the enlightenment, empowerment, and emancipation of the people: people are enlightened when they obtain empirical knowledge about their states of oppression and their potential capacity to improve their situations, people are empowered when they are galvanized to engage in a socially transformation action, people are emancipated when they know who they are, what they genuinely want, and when they have collective autonomy and power to freely and rationally determine the nature and course of their collective existence.	Must raise the people's awareness of their current oppression; must demonstrate the possibility of a qualitatively different future; must hold community members responsible for actively getting involved and creating their own liberation.
Situational Crime Prevention / Crime Prevention Through Environmental Design	SCP is a crime prevention strategy that attempts to eliminate or reduce the opportunities to commit specific crimes in specific locations by making crime more risky to attempt and more difficult to accomplish. Instead of relying upon law enforcers, the SCP strategy depends on public and private organizations. Furthermore, SCP does not focus on the persons committing the crimes or the underlying causes of crime, such as unjust social and economic conditions, but focuses instead on the settings for crime.	Only protects a limited geographical area; crime may be displaced.
Developmental Pathways	Anti-social behaviors are age dependent; as children age, they develop verbal coping skills, which help them manage conflict.	Fails to explain free choice in human development.

Delinquent Development Theory	Persistence in crime is influenced by many risk factors, such as broken homes, low family income, and harsh discipline. Desistance in crime has four factors: deceleration, specialization, de-escalation, and reaching a ceiling (plateau).	Aging causing desistance is meaningless because the theory fails to explain why desistance occurs.
Peacemaking Criminology	Crime can be managed, not by stopping crime, but by making peace; citizens and social control agencies need to work together through education, social policies, human rights, and community involvement.	Is utopian and fails to recognize the realities of law enforcement and crime control limitations.
Feminist Criminology	Men have dominated the field of criminal justice and have developed theories and written laws for the explanation and control of crime based on their own limited perspectives.	Inadequately accounts for crimes committed by females. Currently there is no single well-developed theory that explains female crime.

Conclusion: Why Theory Is Important

Theories help explain problems and provide possible solutions to the problems. However, all theories rely on assumptions, which may impact the effectiveness of decisions based on those theories. Understanding criminal theories is important because police officers need to make best-practice decisions to solve current problems. Applying the wrong theory to solve the problem at hand will be less than optimal. As stated earlier, this is why Megan's Law is proving to be less than effective. According to research on Megan's Law, the deterrence theory and labeling theory are being used to solve a biological-based problem (Corrigan, 2006). Thus, the proposed solution is not in alignment with the theories used to explain the problem and, consequently, Megan's Law is not effectively working.

Theories also control the types of questions that should be asked on research surveys. Data collecting surveys need to ask questions that are in alignment with the theory used to describe the problem. Otherwise the survey itself may not be valid. For example, if the biological theory is used to explain a problem, it does not make sense to ask questions about social learning experiences. For the instrument to be effective, it must collect information that is relevant to the study.

In short, every criminal theory has a limitation and there is always an exception to the rule when trying to explain human behavior. Law enforcers must understand the various limitations of information so that they can defend their actions. Understanding information will also help prevent police officers from being deceived. **In order to assess risk and vulnerability, the law enforcer must understand information.**

Questions to ponder….

Q1: Why does the sky get dark at night?

As previously discussed, if you believe that the sky gets dark at night because the sun is on the other side of the earth, then you have made a flawed assumption (Verma, 2005). The flawed assumption is that the sun is the only light in the sky and that the lack of sunlight causes darkness. Getting dark at night and the sun being on the other side of the earth are correlated, but it is not causal relationship. **There is another reason why it gets dark at night.** Thus, a research based on wrong assumptions may produce poor results. Therefore, students should always assess the validity of information by asking certain questions. Some of the factors that should be evaluated include a) the data collection process, b) the data analysis, c) the participants, d) the assumptions, and e) the limitations.

Divide into groups and each group attempt to answer this question:

Q2: I have three coins, which total 25 cents. However, one of them is not a nickel. What are the three coins? Clue: one of them is not a nickel ≠ not one of them is a nickel.

References

Adams, W. (1999). The interpermeation of self and world: Empirical research, existential phenomenology, and transpersonal psychology. *Journal of Phenomenological Psychology, 30*(2), 39-65.

American Psychological Association. (2010). *Publication manual of the American Psychological Association* (6th ed.). Washington, DC: Author.

Balian, E.S. (1988). *How to design, analyze, and write doctoral or master's research* (2nd ed.). New York, NY: University Press of America.

Corrigan, R. (2006). Making meaning of Megan's law. *Law & Social Inquiry*, 31(2), 267-312.

Fay, B. (1987). *Critical social science*. Ithaca, NY: Cornell University Press.

Huesmann, L.R., & Eron, L.D. (1992). Childhood aggression and adult criminality. In J. McCord (Ed.), *Facts, frameworks, and forecasts: Advances in criminology theory* (p. 137-156). New Brunswick, NJ: Transaction.

Huesmann, L.R., Eron, L.D., & Dubow, E.F. (2002). Childhood predictors of adult criminality: Are all risk factors reflected in childhood aggressiveness? *Criminal Behaviour and Mental Health, 12*(3), 185-208.

Langevin, R., Curnoe, S., Federoff, P., Bennett, R., Langevin, M., Peever, C., et al. (2004). Lifetime sex offender recidivism: A 25-year follow-up study. *Canadian Journal of Criminology and Criminal Justice*, 46(5), 531-552.

Large, T. (2006). *The Usborne illustrated dictionary of math*. London, England: Usborne.

Leedy, P., & Ormrod, J. (2005). *Practical research: Planning and design* (8th ed.). Upper Saddle River, NJ: Pearson Merrill Prentice Hall.

LexisNexis (2005). *Immigration law handbook*. Longwood, FL: Gould.

Miller-Johnson, S., Moore, B.L., Underwood, M.K., & Cole, J.D. (2005). African-American girls and physical aggression: Does stability of childhood aggression predict later negative outcomes? In D. Pepler, K. Madsen, C. Webster, & K. Levene (Eds.), *The development and treatment of girlhood aggression* (p. 75-101). Mahwah, NJ: Lawrence Erlbaum.

Ponterotto, J. (2005). Qualitative research in counseling psychology: A primer on research paradigms and philosophy of science. *Journal of Counseling, 52*(2), 126-136.

Schmalleger, F. (2011). *Criminology: A brief introduction.* Boston, MA: Prentice Hall

Shields, L. (2007). Falsification. *Pediatric Nursing,* 19(7), 37.

Smith, S., Eggen, M., St. Andre, R. (2006). *A transition to advanced mathematics* (6th ed.). Belmont, CA: Thomson Brooks/Cole.

Sower, C., & Gist, G.T. (1994). *Formula for change: Using the urban experiment station methods and the normative sponsorship theory.* East Lansing, MI: Michigan State University Press.

Sower, C., Holland, J., Tiedke, K., & Freeman, W. (1957). *Community Involvement: The webs of formal and informal ties that make for action.* Glencoe, IL: The Free Press.

Turvey, B. E., & Petherick, W. (2009). *Forensic victimology: Examining violent crime victims in   investigative and legal contexts.* Burlington, MA: Academic Press.

Verma, S. (2005). The little book of scientific principles, theories, & things. New York, NY: Sterling.

Vold, G., Bernard, T., and Snipes, J. (2002). *Theoretical criminology* (5th ed.). New York, NY: Oxford University Press.

Wakefield, W. (1995). When an irresistible epistemology meets an immovable ontology. *Social Work Research, 19*(1).

Zevitz, R.G. (2006). Sex offender community notification: Its role in recidivism and offender reintegration. *Criminal Justice Studies,* 19(2), 193-208.

CHAPTER 7. VARIABLES

When working in the field of criminal justice, we need to be able to understand the strengths and weaknesses of research and the impact that a variety of variables can have on a situation or a study. A variable is a quantity or characteristic that has two or more possible values and is not constant or fixed (Leedy & Ormrod, 2005). There are four scales of measurement for variables, which are **nominal, ordinal, interval,** and **ratio**. See *Table 9*. For practical purposes, the distinction between ratio and interval scales is seldom important in statistical analysis (Norusis, 2008). Thus, the **Scale** variable may be used to simply represent a continuous variable, which may be either an interval or ratio variable. It is important to define the variables correctly at the beginning of a research study because the definitions will impact the data analysis. Although higher scale variables can be redefined into lower scale variables, lower scale variables cannot be redefined into higher scale variables.

Table 9

Scales of Measurement (Field, 2005; Leedy & Ormrod, 2005)

Variable Types		
Categorical	**Nominal**	Categories without quantitative measurement and without rank. Examples: male or female; number on a sports uniform; democrat or republican; property record & receipt #; social security #.
	Ordinal	Categories with rank but without a precise difference between each data value. Examples: much or few; rich or poor; like or dislike; fast or slow; hot or cold; birth order; military rank; young or old.
Continuous **Scale**	**Interval**	Data with rank and an equal unit of measurement between each data value, but with no true zero point. Examples: sea level; actual degrees in Celsius; actual IQ scores.
	Ratio	Data with rank and an equal unit of measurement between each data value with a true zero point. Examples: age in actual number of years; actual percentage points; actual number of crimes.

Variable Definitions on Data Analysis

This section does not deal with calculating statistics. It is about knowing what statistic to use in a particular study. Computer programs can easily perform the calculations. See *Table 10* for variable definitions and concerns.

Table 10

Variables & Multicollinearity

Term	Description
Variable	Quantity or characteristic that has two or more possible values (Leedy, P., & Ormrod, 2005).
Dependent Variable (Outcome Variable)	Its value is influenced by any other variables. Its value is usually not manipulated by the researcher (Field, 2005).
Independent Variable (Predictor Variable)	Its value is not influenced by any other variables. Its value is usually manipulated by the researcher to see its impact on other variables (Field, 2005).
Extraneous variables	The factors other than the predictor variables that may influence the dependent variable (Warner, 2008).
Interaction Variables	Although several independent variables may uniquely impact the dependent variable, they may also interact with one another and produce a combined impact on the output that is greater than any additive combination of their separate effects (Cohen & Cohen, 1983; Neuman, 2006; Norusis, 2008).
Multicollinearity	When variables overlap and explain the same thing; it poses a threat to validity because the contribution of each variable is not accurate.

In performing quantitative research, the researcher needs to select the proper statistical test to perform. Each type of statistical test relies on assumptions and has limitations. Selecting the wrong statistical test will impact the interpretation of the outcome. In short, the researcher must articulate why the particular test was selected and disclose its limitations.

Tables 11-14 may help guide a researcher in selecting the appropriate statistical test. The first chart involves examining relationships or differences between the independent and dependent variables (Salkind, 2007). The second chart involves the nature of the outcome variables (Field, 2005). The purpose of the charts is to provide a guide for selecting the correct statistical method. It is up to the researcher to verify the correct statistical method. For example, if the guide indicates to conduct multiple regression analysis, this is not good enough because there are three different types of multiple regression analysis. Thus, the researcher must verify and articulate the correct method by examining the method in more detail. Blindly relying on the guide is insufficient to effectively defend the statistic employed. Remember, it is only a guide that may be used to point the researcher in the right direction. The researcher must investigate further.

Each statistical test will depend upon a) the scales of measurement of the variables, b) the number of predictor variables, and c) the number of outcome variables. Parametric statistics are more powerful than nonparametric statistics (Norusis, 2008). Parametric statistics use higher scales of measurement (i.e., ratio and interval) for data, which can provide more detailed information than nonparametric statistics, which use nominal or ordinal data. If parametric assumptions are met, then parametric statistics should take precedence over nonparametric statistics. However, although nonparametric statistics ignore some of the available information, they can be useful if outliers exist that affect the mean (average). Indeed, nonparametric statistics will not be as easily influenced by outliers as will parametric tests because nonparametric statistics use median and rank values instead of actual values. Thus, although nonparametric statistics may not be as good at finding differences in the data when the parametric assumptions have been met, they can be very good when there are serious departures from the parametric assumptions.

The type of statistical analysis that can effectively be performed on data will be determined by how the scales of measurement for the variables are defined (i.e., nominal, ordinal, interval, ratio). In other words, if the variables are defined incorrectly, then the researcher will be limited in the type of statistics that may be used to assess the data. Therefore, research variables should be defined in advance so that the desired statistical analysis can be performed. Indeed, researchers need to look at what they are trying to accomplish and they should collect data in the correct format so that the can accomplish their objective. Just because data are collected does not mean that any statistical test can effectively be performed on the data.

Once the data are collected, descriptive statistical analyses need to be performed. For example, if the variables have been classified as continuous variables, then they need to be assessed in order to determine if the parametric assumptions have been satisfied. If the parametric assumptions have not been satisfied, then the data may have to be manipulated in order to satisfy the requirements. If the requirements cannot be satisfied, then the data may need to be reconfigured into nonparametric classifications so that nonparametric tests can be performed. In short, parametric statistics are preferred over nonparametric statistics because parametric statistics provide more detailed information (Norusis, 2008).

Research is a systematic process of collecting, analyzing, and interpreting information in order to better understand the subject of study (Leedy & Ormrod, 2005). Research attempts to resolve a problem by answering a question. Researchers communicate their thoughts, objectives, methods, and data interpretation for other people to evaluate and act upon. Researchers accomplish this by developing a hypothesis, which is an educated conjecture, and determining if the data support the hypothesis. In short, the purpose of research is to add to the body of knowledge.

Research begins with an unanswered question and a problem. The researcher clearly defines the problem in the form of a statement. For a quantitative study, a hypothesis must be written so that it includes the variables being tested. The scales of measurement for the independent and dependent variables will determine the proper statistical tests that should be performed.

Table 11

Determining the Appropriate Statistical Test (Field, 2005; Norusis, 2008; Salkind, 2007)

Number of Dependent Variable	Type of Dependent Variables	Number of Independent Variables	Type of Independent Variables	If Categorical independent Variable, Number of Categories	If Categorical independent Variable, Same or Different Participants in Each Category	Parametric Assumptions Satisfied	Appropriate Statistical Test
1	Continuous	1	Categorical	2	Different	Yes	Point-Biserial Correlation or Independent t-test
					Different	No	Mann-Whitney test
					Same	Yes	Dependent *t* test
					Same	No	Wilcoxon Matched-Pairs test
				≥ 3	Different	Yes	One Way Independent ANOVA
					Different	No	Kruskal-Wallis Test
					Same	Yes	One Way Repeated Measures ANOVA
					Same	No	Friedman's ANOVA
			Continuous	-	-	Yes	Regression or Pearson Correlation
						No	Spearman Correlation or Kendall's Tau
		≥ 2	Categorical		Different	Yes	Multiple Regression or Independent Factorial ANOVA
				-	Same	Yes	Factorial Repeated Measures ANOVA
					Both	Yes	Factorial Mixed ANOVA
			Continuous	-	-	Yes	Multiple Regression
			Both	-	-	Yes	Multiple Regression or ANCOVA
	Categorical	1	Categorical	-	Different	-	Pearson Chi-Square or Likelihood Ratio
			Continuous	-	-	-	Logistic Regression, Biserial Correlation, or Point-Biserial Correlation
		≥ 2	Categorical	-	Different	-	Loglinear Analysis
			Continuous	-	-	-	Logistic Regression
			Both	-	Different	-	Logistic Regression
≥ 2	Continuous	1	Categorical	-	-	Yes	MANOVA
		≥ 2	Categorical	-	-	Yes	Factorial MANOVA
			Both	-	-	Yes	MANCOVA

Table 12

Types of Correlational Statistics (Field, 2005; Leedy & Ormrod, 2005; Norusis, 2008)

Types of Correlational Statistics		
	Statistic	Data Description
Parametric Statistic	Pearson correlation	Both variables are continuous
	Coefficient of determination	Both variables are continuous
	Point biserial correlation	One variable = continuous One variable = discrete & dichotomous
	Biserial correlation	One variable = continuous One variable = discrete & dichotomous (with underlying continuum)
	Phi coefficient	Both variables = dichotomies
	Triserial correlation	One variable = continuous One variable = trichotomy
	Partial Correlation	Assessing the relationship between 2 variables when a 3rd variable is held statistically constant.
	Multiple regression	Predicting an outcome by a linear combination of ≥ 2 independent variables.
	Weibull distribution	Test-to-failure analysis; continuous probability distribution. Predicts how long a product will survive at a given confidence level. Good for very low volume.
Nonparametric Statistic	Spearman's rho	Both variables are rank-ordered.
	Kendall coefficient	Both variables are rank-ordered and the statistic assesses their degree of similarity.
	Contingency coefficient	Both variables are nominal.
	Kendall's Tau correlation	Both variables are ordinal and the statistic is useful with a small sample size.

Table 13

Types of Inferential Statistics (Field, 2005; Leedy & Ormrod, 2005; Norusis, 2008)

	Types of Inferential Statistics	
	Statistic	Purpose of Test
Parametric Statistic	Student t test	To determine the difference between 2 means
	Analysis of variance (ANOVA)	To determine the differences among 3 or more means by comparing variances across and within groups. If significant, may also require a post hoc test.
	Analysis of Covariance (ANCOVA)	To determine the differences among means while controlling for the impact of a variable that is related to the outcome variable.
	Regression	To determine how effectively one or more variables predict the outcome variable.
	Factor analysis	To determine the correlations among many variables and to identify highly interrelated variables that reflect themes.
	Structural equation modeling (SEM)	To determine the correlations among many variables in order to determine casual relationships.
Nonparametric Statistic	Sign test	To determine if the values of one variable are larger than the values of a correlated variable.
	Mann-Whitney U	It is used to compare two groups when the variables are ordinal.
	Kruskal-Wallis	It is used to compare ≥ 3 groups when the variables are ordinal.
	Wilcoxon matched-pair	It is used to compare two groups when a relationship exists between the samples and the variables are ordinal.
	Chi-square goodness-of-fit	It is used to compare observed values with predicted values.
	Odds ratio	It is used to assess whether 2 dichotomous nominal variables are correlated.
	Fisher's exact	It is used with a small sample size to assess whether 2 dichotomous nominal or ordinal variables are correlated.

Table 14

Determining Proper Statistic (Salkind, 2007)

Is the research study a test of differences or a test of relationships?						
Test of **Differences** Between Variables					Test of **Relationships** Between Variables	
Same participants being tested more than once?					Number of variables	
Yes		No				
2 groups	≥ 3 groups	2 groups	≥ 3 groups		2 variables	≥ 3 variables
t test for dependent samples	related measures ANOVA	*t* test for independent samples	One factor	≥ 2 factors	*t* test for significance of the correlation coefficient	Factor analysis, regression, or canonical analysis
			simple ANOVA	factorial analysis of variance		

133

Exercises – Variables, Assumptions, Conditional Statements, & Quantifiers

1) You are a nurse. You need to ask the patient how often she takes her medicine. Ask the question three different ways by using a nominal variable, an ordinal variable, and a ratio variable.

2) You are a nurse. You ask the patient if she takes her medicine as prescribed. The patient states that she has not missed a dosage. Evaluate her response.

3) Mark wants to make a $1,000 bet with you that he can accurately guess the score of the next Super Bowl before the game begins. Is this a good bet?

4) James claimed that he was ripped off yesterday by Ralph. James claims that Ralph sold him a Roman coin dated 27 B.C for $5,000, which he guaranteed was authentic. Today, James believes that the coin is significantly less than the market value of $5,000. Was a crime committed?

5) A man claims that he can knock down a brick wall with his bare hands within 10 minutes. Would you consider this man a physical threat for law enforcement purposes?

6) You are a clean-environment supporter. For an $800 investment, you can own the design drawings for a solar powered clothes driver. Is this a good investment?

7) All arrests are by definition seizures. However, are all seizures considered to be arrests? Explain.

8) Signs on the side of the road read, "Speed controlled by Radar." However, an officer stated that he clocked you over the speed limit by using LASER. The officer issues you a citation for excessive speed. Do you have a good defense in court? Explain.

References

Cohen, J, & Cohen, P. (1983). *Applied multiple regression/correlation analysis for the behavioral science* (2nd ed.). Hillsdale, NJ: Lawrence Erlbaum.

Field, A. (2005). *Discovering statistics using SPSS* (2nd ed.). Thousand Oaks, CA: Sage Publications.

Leedy, P., & Ormrod, J. (2005). *Practical research: Planning and design* (8th ed.). Upper Saddle River, NJ: Pearson Merrill Prentice Hall.

Neuman, W.L. (2006). *Social research methods: Qualitative and quantitative approaches* (6th ed.). Boston, MA: Pearson.

Norusis, M.J. (2008). *SPSS 16.0 guide to data analysis.* Upper saddle River, NJ: Prentice Hall.

Salkind, N.J. (2007). *Statistics for people who (think they) hate statistics* (Excel ed.). Thousand Oaks, CA: Sage.

Warner, R.M. (2008). *Applied statistics from bivariate through multivariate techniques.* Los Angeles, CA: Sage Publications.

CHAPTER 8. RELIABILITY, VALIDITY, & ERROR

Good decisions require good data. When performing our criminal justice duties, it is imperative that our decisions and policies are based on solid supporting evidence (data). All research collects some type of data (Balian, 1988). Primary data are data collected specifically for the current study; secondary data are data not collected specifically for the current study. The validity and reliability of the data must be assessed for both primary and secondary data. If the data are valid, then the data are reliable. However, if the data are reliable does not mean that the data are valid. See *Table 15*. In other words, the converse of a conditional statement is not necessarily true.

Reliability = consistency

Validity = true and accurate information; measures what it is supposed to measure

An alarm clock that is 30 minutes slow every day is reliable. However, it is consistently wrong. Thus, just because data is reliable does not make the data valid.

Table 15
Reliability & Validity (Balian, 1988)

Actual Time (True Data)	Valid = Yes Reliable = Yes	Valid = No Reliable = Yes	Valid = No Reliable = No
1:00 pm	1:00 pm	1:30 pm	1:00 pm
2:00 pm	2:00 pm	2:30 pm	2:11 pm
3:00 pm	3:00 pm	3:30 pm	3:24 pm
4:00 pm	4:00 pm	4:30 pm	5:03 pm

Research instruments are used to collect data. Consequently, the validity of the instruments needs to be assessed. Because there are many variables in life, it may be hard to determine if an instrument is actually measuring what it is supposed to measure.

Validity

Basically, there are three types of validity that need to be assessed for an instrument: content validity, criterion-related validity, and construct validity (Balian, 1988). Content validity is a subjective approach, criterion validity is an objective approach, and construct validity is a combination of the subjective and objective approach. See *Table 16*.

Table 16
Types of Validity (Balian, 1988; Salkind, 2007)

Type of Validity	Pros	Cons
Content Validity	Easy to implement; Easy to understand; No statistics required; Fast, cheap	Lack of statistical analysis; Depends on opinions
Concurrent/Predictive Validity	Statistically objective; Widely used, accepted; Easy to calculate; Fast, if concurrent; Can be cheap (depends on number of participants)	Power of statistical analysis depends on criteria used; May take a long time, if predictive; Can be costly (depends on number of participants)
Construct Validity	Sophisticated statistics; Fast results (computer analysis); Provides more complete information	Requires many instrument questions and participants; Difficult to learn; Difficult to explain; May be expensive (depends on number of participants and software used)

Content validity is a subjective way to assess validity (Balian, 1988). This method uses opinions and judgments to determine if the instrument measures what it is supposed to measure. Experts or a formal panel of judges may evaluate an instrument's questions and the researcher may add or drop questions based on that information. Using a panel of judges may be more credible than using the sole opinion of one person. Although not scientific in its approach, content validity can be valuable in certain research situations. In addition, other validity methods may be used in conjunction with content validity in order to enhance the overall validity of the instrument.

Criterion-related validity is determined by creating correlation coefficients (Balian, 1988). There are two common types of criterion-related validity: concurrent validity, and predictive validity. For example, if a researcher develops an instrument, the researcher may determine the validity of the new instrument by comparing it to a published instrument (the criterion), which is supposed to measure the same information. In this case, the researcher may provide both instruments (the new and published instrument) to the sample and the sample's responses to both instruments will be statistically compared by determining a correlation coefficient. The closer the correlation coefficient is to +1.00, the more valid is the instrument.

The researcher may then use the new instrument to collect data over time (Balian, 1988). The researcher may compare a participant's current score on the new instrument to the participant's future score on the new instrument to assess the correlation coefficient between select variables. If there is a relationship between the current scores and the scores collected in the future, then the researcher must determine the strength of the relationship. The strength of the relationship is described by the correlation coefficient. The range of coefficient magnitude is 0 – 1 and closer the correlation coefficient is to +1.00, the stronger is the relationship. Negative coefficients indicate a negative relationship. Thus, the researcher may be able to use the new instrument to predict future events. This is predictive validity.

It must be noted that although a correlation between two instruments may exist, it does not mean that the instruments are measuring what they are supposed to measure. Two instruments may be highly correlated but both instruments may have validity concerns. For example, although a verbal aggression instrument may be highly correlated to a physical aggression instrument, both instruments may have little value for a study related to the type of green beans that a person purchases.

Once a correlation coefficient has been determined, what does the number mean? Below are two scales to determine the strengths of relationships based on the correlation coefficients for criterion-related validity measures (Balian, 1988; Salkind, 2007). See *Table 17*. A researcher should reference the most appropriate information. It is the researcher's responsibility to persuade others that the researcher's actions are most appropriate. Positive coefficients indicate a positive relationship and negative coefficients indicate a negative relationship.

Table 17

Strength of Correlation Coefficient (Balian, 1988; Salkind, 2007)

correlation coefficient	relationship	correlation coefficient	relationship
1.0 - .90	excellent	1.0 - .8	very strong
.89 - .80	good	.6 - .8	strong
.79 - .70	fair	.4 -.6	moderate
.69 or less	poor	.2 -.4	weak
		.0 - .2	weak or none
(Balian, 1988)		(Salkind, 2007)	

Construct Validity is the highest form of validity and uses multivariate factor analysis to develop factors (constructs) within each instrument (Balian, 1988). For example, an instrument used to measure aggression may be broken down into specific types of aggression, each type being a construct. The aggression instrument may be broken down into a) physical aggression, b) verbal aggression, c) indirect aggression, d) anger, and e) hostility. If a specific type of aggression is detected, then corrective actions may focus on that type of aggression.

For a new instrument, the researcher can assess the interrelations between the questions (Balian, 1988). Construct validity improves as the number of questions and respondents increase. When the respondents answer questions, relations among the answers are determined. Thus, the respondents determine the constructs and not the researcher.

Reliability

An instrument is reliable if it is consistent in its measurements (Balian, 1988). See *Table 18* for different types of reliability. Like validity coefficients, the range of coefficient magnitude is $0 - 1$ and closer the correlation coefficient is to $+1.00$, the stronger is the relationship. Negative coefficients indicate a negative relationship. Some common reliability techniques include a) test-retest reliability, b) split-half reliability, c) equivalent forms reliability, and d) internal consistency reliability.

Test-Retest

A survey instrument is administered to the same group of participants at two different points in time (Balian, 1988). If the survey is consistent, then the responses should be the same at the two different times. A correlation coefficient is calculated between the participants' first and second scores. The correlation may be determined for the item score or for the total score. However, the test-retest may produce spurious results due to practice effects. This reliability test should only be performed when other methods are not feasible.

Split-Half

The Split-Half reliability test is an enhanced variation of the test-retest reliability procedure (Balian, 1988). All of the survey items are placed in order of difficulty (for cognitive surveys) or by subject matter (if attitudinal survey). The items are numbered and then split into two groups. One group (test A) will consist of the even numbered items and the other group (test B) will consist of the odd numbered items. If the instrument is reliable, then the scores on the two surveys should be highly correlated. The assumption is that the two tests are relatively equal in content and difficulty. Because the surveys are only administered at one time, this procedure is cost effective.

Equivalent Forms

For the equivalent forms method, two completely separate but equal surveys are created (Balian, 1988). The same participants are surveyed twice, once for each survey. If the instruments are reliable, then the scores on the two surveys will be highly correlated. This method requires many questions, it may be costly, and creating similar surveys can be difficult.

Internal Consistency

Internal consistency techniques utilize more sophisticated statistics to determine reliability coefficients (Balian, 1988). The theory behind this technique indicates that each item on the survey should be answered in the same direction as the total score direction. Although this method only needs to be implemented once, it may require many survey items (the more, the better).

Table 18
Types of Reliability (Balian, 1988)

Type of Reliability	Pros	Cons
Test-Retest	Easy to use; Easy to understand	Take much time; Costly; Practice effect in respondents
Split-Half	One test administration; Easy to understand	May be difficult to split test
Equivalent Forms	Two separate tests	Takes much time; Hard to write equivalent test items; May be costly
Internal Consistency	Statistically most sophisticated; Well respected; May provide much information	Hard to understand; Hard to explain

Type I & Type II Error

Because human knowledge is limited, null hypotheses cannot actually be proved true (Shields, 2007). For example, we will never know for sure if any of the many extraneous variables have impacted a particular relationship between known variables. Thus, because relationships cannot be proved true, an attempt is made to prove them false. There are two types of error in quantitative research (Leedy & Ormrod, 2005). One error occurs when researchers accept information as true when it is actually false (Type II). The other type of error occurs when researchers reject information as false when it is really true (Type I). There is a tradeoff between these two types of errors. Indeed, when one error decreases, the other one increases. Because a sample is being evaluated and not the entire population, the researcher cannot know for certainty which error will be made. Thus, to ensure that the null hypothesis is not wrongly rejected when it is actually true, the alpha level can be set extremely low in order to minimize making the Type 1 error. In other words, if we make a

142

mistake, we would rather say that it is true that there is no relationship rather than to say that it is false that there is no relationship. After all, we are trying to show that there is a relationship and it would more conservative to say that we did not prove our point.

In the courtroom, the null hypothesis states that there is no relationship between the defendant and the commission of the crime. The defense attorney will want to advocate an alpha level of zero, which indicates that there is no possibility of making a Type 1 error (which means that there is zero chance of convicting an innocent person; in fact, no one will ever be convicted). On the other hand, the prosecutor will want to advocate an alpha level of 100%, which means that there is no chance of making a Type 2 error (which means that there is zero chance of releasing a guilty person; in fact, all will be found guilty).

In a courtroom setting, the jury needs some sort of reference (i.e., alpha level) for the determination of guilt. If the jury determines that a 95% confidence level is sufficient for a guilty verdict, then, if a mistake is made, the jury is willing to wrongly convict an innocent person 5% of the time and to release a guilty person 95% of the time. Thus, in this case, it is more important not to convict an innocent person than to release a guilty person. It is obvious that mistakes are expected in the U.S. legal system.

A commonly used alpha level in academic research is .05 and it is determined prior to collecting any data (Leedy & Ormrod, 2005). Once the alpha level has been determined, the researcher cannot be allowed to subjectively adjust the alpha level. If this were allowed to happen, then where will the line be drawn? If .051 is acceptable, then what about .052, .053, .054, etc.? Thus, standards need to be absolute. Whenever a line is drawn, there will be cases near each other on either side of the line. However, functionally indistinguishable values on opposite sides of the line do not invalidate the line. Thus, absolute standards are essential for providing consistency and credibility to a study.

Cause and effect relationship between the variables may be challenged because there may be many extraneous variables that may impact the dependent variables (Bordens &

Abbott, 2008). If the temporal precedence of the variables is ambiguous, then the relationship can only be claimed to be correlational and not claimed to be causal. For example, do smart kids participate in after-school activities, or do after-school activities make kids smart? By tightening the control over the extraneous variables, a study's validity will improve.

The internal validity of a study will be threatened to the extent that the extraneous variables can provide alternate explanations for the findings (Bordens & Abbott, 2008). Basically, the only way to determine a cause and effect relationship is to perform a true experimental study. Simply observing that a change in one variable is accompanied by a change in another variable is not enough to establish causation. For example, there are many factors that may affect a person's life, such as family interactions and educational opportunities, which may affect a study's results. Thus, it may be very difficult to control and account for all of the variables that may impact the results.

References

Balian, E.S. (1988). *How to design, analyze, and write doctoral or master's research* (2nd ed.). New York, NY: University Press of America.

Bordens, K., & Abbott, B. (2008). *Research design and methods: A process approach* (7th ed.). Boston, MA: McGraw Hill.

Leedy, P., & Ormrod, J. (2005). *Practical research: Planning and design* (8th ed.). Upper Saddle River, NJ: Pearson Merrill Prentice Hall.

Salkind, N.J. (2007). *Statistics for people who (think they) hate statistics* (Excel ed.). Thousand Oaks, CA: Sage.

Shields, L. (2007). Falsification. *Pediatric Nursing*, 19(7), 37.

CHAPTER 9. AN EXAMPLE OF ISSUES IN A RESEARCH STUDY

Following is an example of some of the issues that are involved with research and information gathering. It is important to understand that there can be many concerns with any study. Students should never take the findings of a study at face value. Students should always challenge the validity of any study. If the researcher fails to disclose vital information, then the study is suspect and should not be accepted as valid. This is the reason why scholarly peer-reviewed studies are very credible sources of information. To be published in a peer-reviewed scholarly journal, other experts in the field assess the study to determine if the study is credible and worthy of publication. Thus, there is much more scrutiny and many more barriers to overcome for a scholarly peer-reviewed publication than for a publication that is not required to be scrutinized by experts in the field.

To provide an idea of some of the assumptions and limitations associated with a research study, part of a research study will be reviewed. The title of the study is *"A Correlational Study of Childhood Religiosity, Childhood Sport Participation, and Sport-Learned Aggression among African American Female Athletes"* (Davis, 2011).

Purpose of Study

The purpose of the study was to quantitatively examine if there is a significant relationship among youth contact sports participation, childhood religiosity, and aggressive behaviors later in life. Because childhood aggression has been linked to adult criminality, and because sport participation has been linked to aggression, there was a need to study childhood sport-learned aggression. The researcher felt that before the bigger problem of adult criminality can be resolved, the factors related to learned aggression must be better understood. Therefore, this particular study employed a correlational survey design, collected data using a non-random and purposive sample, and used multiple regression analysis to assess the relationships among youth contact sport participation, childhood religiosity, and aggressive behaviors later in life.

Theory Concerns and Validation

According to social learning theory, the behaviors of athletes are reinforced over time according to the intensity, duration, and frequency of social learning experiences (Akers & Sellers, 2009). However, although aggression is present in contact sports, not all athletes perceive aggression in the same way. On one hand, some athletes may perceive aggression in contact sports in a positive manner; consequently, they may learn self-discipline and organizational skills. On the other hand, some athletes may perceive aggression in contact sports in a negative manner; consequently, they may learn to hurt and control other people. In addition, childhood religiosity, another social learning experience, may impact how behaviors in contact sports are perceived and may influence the behaviors learned during contact sports participation. In this study the researcher examines the data collected to see if the research assumption holds up against the information actually collected.

First, the researcher needs to conduct a thorough review of other peer reviewed sources to identify the criticisms of the social learning theory. For example, the social learning theory states that the same learning process produces both conforming and nonconforming behaviors (Akers & Sellers, 2009). Thus, what is actually learned in any given situation depends on the learning process within each individual. Because pro-social behaviors are culturally determined, whether a person perceives a role model to be positive or negative is relative. Therefore, the researcher must understand the background of the person under investigation in order to properly understand what that person is learning. Because America is a mosaic of different cultures, the actual behaviors learned by different individuals in any given situation are questionable. In short, making generalizations about specific groups or theories may be problematic.

Second, although social learning theorists believe that exterior forces influence interior behavior, they fail to consider cognitive development (Durkin, 1995). Indeed, social learning theorists emphasize internal cognitive processes and assume that the information processing capacities of individuals change with experience and maturity. However, they resist "the notion of general structural reorganizations as a response to conflicts between developing understanding and empirical discovers" (Durkin, p. 25).

Third, social learning theorists dismiss biological factors and they place too much emphasis on situational factors (Durkin, 1995). For example, social learning theorists fail to address the nature of human emotions. Indeed, they dismiss the notion that personality traits may be a major feature of social behavior.

Fourth, rewards, punishments, and reinforcements, which are central to the social learning theory, are poorly defined (Durkin, 1995). In fact, they are tautological. For example, a person may define something as reinforcing simply because the person finds it reinforcing. Thus, the social learning theory does not provide a true explanation of behavior (Bordens & Abbott, 2008). Being aware of this one point may change how the researcher examines the data collected.

Finally, the social learning theory is "limited in its conception of social context and social influences" (Durkin, 1995, p. 26). Specifically, aside from modeling and reinforcement, the social learning theory fails to adequately consider a) how other people help an individual construct the social world, b) how the individual acquires shared representations of social and interpersonal phenomena, and c) how some developmental routes are encouraged and some are inhibited as a result of particular social arrangements.

Even though we have seen that social learning theory has several criticisms, there is a large body of evidence that provides strong and consistent support for Akers' social learning theory (Akers, 2009; Hwang & Akers, 2003). In an effort to personally validate the social learning theory, Akers surveyed 3,065 adolescents in order to determine the relationship between drug and alcohol abuse and the social learning variables (Siegel,

2003). The findings indicated that there is a strong association between individuals who believed that they would be rewarded by someone that they respected for their deviant acts and the likelihood that they would perform those deviant acts. Furthermore, the findings indicated that individuals who commit deviant acts seek out other individuals who also commit deviant acts as a means for support and companionship. Akers (2009) demonstrated that the findings of his study strongly supported the variables of his social learning theory. In short, best practice decisions require complete information, which requires both the pros and cons of the theory. Only by thoroughly examining a wide variety of viewpoints can a researcher gain a decent perspective on the research topic.

Sample Size

If the sample truly represents the population being studied, then a larger sample will provide more reliable results. However, there is a point where additional participants will add very little additional information relevant to the population. For example, for a 95% confidence level with a 5% confidence interval, a population of 100 will need a sample size of 80, a population of 1,000 will need a sample size of 278, a population of 10,000 will need a sample size of 370, a population of 100,000 will need a sample size of 383, and a population of 1,000,000 will need a sample size of 384 (Creative Research Systems, 2010).

However, if the sample is not representative of the population, which may occur during the collection of large samples, such as when the census is taken, a larger sample size may produce less accurate results than if a smaller and more representative sample is recruited. For example, many undocumented persons may not be considered in the census and this may bias the results; hence, a smaller and more representative sample may be more accurate. A larger sample will provide more solid information, but if the sample is biased then the results will be more solidly biased away from the true population. Several questions that we need to ask about any study include a) what are the characteristics of the participants, b) did the sample accurately represent the population being studied, and c) what was sample size? If the answers to these questions are unclear, the study has serious flaws.

Parametric Assumptions

Multiple regression is a parametric statistic, which requires that several assumptions be satisfied (Norusis, 2008). First, multiple regression requires that the independent variables be either continuous or categorical and that the dependent variable be continuous (Field, 2005). Second, the sample size must be adequate (Tabachnick & Fidel, 2007). Third, the observations must be independent from one another (Norusis). Fourth, the errors terms must be independent from one another, which indicate that the order of the survey responses did not impact the variability of the responses (Tabachnick & Fidel). Fifth, there must be sampling normality, which indicates that the samples upon which the data are collected are from populations that are approximately normally distributed and that have scores that are normally distributed (Bordens & Abbott, 2008). Sixth, the variance of the criterion variable must be the same for all values of the independent variable (Norusis). Finally, the dependent variable must have a linear relationship with the independent variables.

Assumptions of the Study

There are several assumptions in the study. First, the researcher assumes that the participants have completed the surveys themselves and that they have reported truthful responses. In order to help manage the problem, a large sample size has been targeted, which will help identify outliers (Field, 2005; Norusis, 2008). Second, for organized school-sponsored contact sports in the U.S., the researcher assumes that the participants have experienced similar social learning experiences. In other words, student athletes all across the country are subjected to similar operant conditioning in the development of similar competitive behaviors. Finally, in accordance with the social learning theory, pro-social and anti-social behaviors are assumed to be learned through the same cognitive and behavioral mechanisms, learning is assumed to be an on-going process, and various social learning experiences are assumed to influence one another (Hwang & Akers, 2003). Because pro-social behaviors are culturally determined, whether a person perceives a role model to be positive or negative is relative. Therefore, the researcher must understand the background of the person under investigation in order to properly understand what that person is learning. Due to the United States being a mosaic of different cultures, the actual behaviors learned by different individuals in any given situation are questionable.

Interaction Variable

Although two independent variables may uniquely impact the dependent variable, they may also interact with one another and produce a combined impact on the output that is greater than any additive combination of their separate effects (Cohen & Cohen, 1983; Neuman, 2006; Norusis, 2008). The interaction between two independent variables may be significant if the importance of one independent variable varies over the range of the other independent variable (Tabachnick & Fidell, 2007).

However, when considering the interaction effect, it may not be optimal to consider all possible combinations of the independent variables (Norusis, 2008). First, considering too many interaction variables may a) harm the accuracy of the regression model and b) reduce its predictive capability (Cohen and Cohen, 1983). Second, the study's hypotheses may not warrant testing for multiple interaction relationships. Third, an increased number of hypotheses increases the risk of Type I error (believing that there is a genuine effect when there is not) and increases the risk of failing to detect Type II error (believing that there is no effect when there actually is an effect). Finally, the extraneous variables in a study may not be measured with enough precision to effectively measure interaction relationships. As a result, according to Cohen and Cohen (1993), no interaction variables should be included in an analysis unless there is substantial evidence to believe that they should be included or unless there is a particular interest in the interaction. Otherwise, the conclusions drawn from the research study may be jeopardized.

151

Multicollinearity

A high multicollinearity between two independent variables poses a threat to the validity of multiple regression (Field, 2005). If two variables have a correlation above .80, then there is most likely a multicollinearity problem (Allison, 1999; Berry & Feldman, 1985; Field). Multicollinearity exists when variables overlap and explain the same thing. Thus, the contribution of each variable is not accurate. For example, living in a poor neighborhood may explain 90% of crime and making a low income may explain 90% of crime. However, they do not explain 180% of the crime when they are considered together. If there is a multicollinearity problem between two variables, then one of the variables should be dismissed.

Multicollinearity exists when independent variables provide redundant information about the behavior of the dependent variable and, consequently, the unique contributions of each independent variable cannot be determined (Kahane, 2008). Moreover, except for extreme cases, multicollinearity is always present to some degree (W. D. Berry & Feldman, 1985; Schroeder et al., 1986). This is a concern because multiple regression is designed to separate the contributions of two or more independent variables on a dependent variable.

There is no best method in handling multicollinearity (Schroeder et al., 1986). Thus, if there is high multicollinearity between two independent variables, then one of the independent variables may need to be eliminated from the regression model (Newton & Rudestam, 1999; Schroeder et al.). This is an acceptable procedure because little information is lost in dropping one of the independent variables. However, the researcher must be aware that dropping an independent variable may compromise the theory behind the regression model (Kahane, 2008).

Limitations of the Study

All studies have limitations. First, if the sample is convenient, purposive, and non-random, then there is the possibility that the participants who choose to participate may be different in meaningful ways from those individuals who choose not to participate. As a result, the findings cannot be generalized to other population groups that do not match the sample's characteristics. Second, a quantitative study does not provide an in-depth understanding of the meanings that the participants have associated with their lived experiences (Berg, 2007). Third, if a study like the one being discussed is based on a correlational design, it might not indicate causal relationships (Bordens & Abbott, 2008). Fourth, if a study has too wide an age span, as this study does in which the sample's age range is 21 to 40 years of age, this allows too much time for other variables to affect some of the participants' aggression levels. For example, some participants may have been exposed to extraneous variables 19 years longer than other participants. Fifth, the researcher must examine other elements happening in the socio-cultural environment that may affect the results. For example in the study being discussed, poor U.S. economic status and the U.S. involvement in a war may be controversial social events that have created anger in sections of the society (Bordens & Abbott, 2008). Indeed, the study's data have been collected from participants at a time when the unemployment rate in the U.S. has been increasing for over two years (U.S. Department of Labor, 2010). Thus, the hardships and social learning experiences that have fallen upon the participants over the last several years may have impacted their aggression levels at the time of the survey. Finally, Likert-type scales were used in this study and there is a possibility that a) the participants engaged in central tendency bias by simply selecting the middle option rather than the best option, b) the participants engaged in acquiescence bias by simply selecting positive responses over negative responses, and c) due to limited options, the participants were forced to select options that did not accurately represent their realities (Antonovich, 2008). However, Likert-type scales have a long history of successful use in the criminal justice field and are quite effective in the collection of a large amount of data in a uniform manner in a short amount of time (Champion, 2006).

Limitations of Crime Statistics

Using crime statistics to assess whether contact sports are linked to crime is also problematic. First, contact sport participation is not a statistic collected on inmates by state and federal correctional authorities (U.S. Department of Justice, 1996; U.S. General Accounting Office, 2000). Thus, there is a lack of data. Second, because athletes are among the most popular individuals in society, their actions may be scrutinized by the media and public (Coakley, 2004). Thus, if athletes commit crimes, then their anti-social activities may be advertised more by the media than the anti-social activities of non-athletes (Miracle & Rees, 1994). Third, it is not possible to know the actual number of crimes committed in society because only about 40% of the crimes are ever reported to the police (B. Berry & Smith, 2000; U.S. Department of Justice, 2010). Thus, crime statistics are incomplete and, consequently, they are less than accurate. Fourth, African Americans are disproportionately found guilty once they are arrested (B. Berry & Smith; Mauer & King, 2007; Walker, Spohn, & DeLone, 2007). As a result, an inflated African American incarceration rate may be generated. Fifth, if aggression is present then there is crime; however, if crime is present does not mean that there is aggression (e.g., there may be other reasons why people are arrested). Indeed, because the converse of a conditional statement is not necessarily true, the process of looking at crime statistics to assess sports-related aggression would be a flawed (S. Smith, Eggen, & St. Andre, 2006). Sixth, school sponsored contact sports may teach athletes to play aggressively, but school sponsored contact sports do not teach children to violate the law. Thus, aggression, and not crime statistics, is the appropriate variable of interest in the study. Finally, there is a logic problem with trying to perform a correlational study involving inmates and their participation in school sponsored contact sports (S. Smith et al.). In other words, the consequence (i.e., incarceration) is always true whether the hypotheses are true or false. Thus, if the consequence is true for every level of contact sport participation, then empirical data cannot be used to test the hypotheses (Neuman, 2006).

154

Extraneous Variables

There are numerous factors other than sport participation and childhood religiosity that may potentially impact learned aggression (Borum, 2000; Connor, 2002; Huesmann, Dubow, & Boxer, 2009; Marcus, 2009; Pepler & Craig, 2005; U.S. Department of Health and Human Services, Office of the Surgeon General, 2001). The factors other than the predictor variables that may influence the dependent variable are called extraneous variables (Warner, 2008). Because multiple regression does not distinguish between predictor variables and extraneous variables, both types of independent variables should be considered (Allison, 1999). However, it is important to only consider relevant extraneous variables and the proper number of extraneous variables (W. D. Berry & Feldman, 1985; Kahane, 2008). Otherwise, specification error (i.e., the wrong model) may result and the regression model may be less than effective in its predicative capability (W. D. Berry & Feldman).

On the one hand, specification error may result if too many extraneous variables are considered (W. D. Berry & Feldman, 1985). Therefore, only the minimum number of relevant extraneous variables should be considered. For example, if extraneous variables that are highly related to the predictor variables are considered, then their inclusion in the regression model may increase the standard error of the estimated coefficients. Consequently, considering too many extraneous variables may seriously impact the regression model and reduce its effectiveness to predict.

On the other hand, specification error may result if too few extraneous variables are considered (W. D. Berry & Feldman, 1985). Indeed, it is important not to exclude a relevant extraneous variable because the estimates of those independent variables left in the equation will become biased. In other words, when a relevant extraneous variable is omitted, the variables left in the regression model that are correlated to the missing extraneous variable will absorb some of the impact that the excluded variable would have

155

had on the dependent variable. Thus, excluding relevant extraneous variables may produce unreliable results (Field, 2005).

The accuracy of the regression model to predict relationships among the independent and dependent variables relies on using relevant extraneous variables (W. D. Berry & Feldman, 1985). Therefore, in an effort to consider enough extraneous variables that measure different aspects of a person's life, while at the same time minimizing the number of extraneous variables that are considered, three major risk factor domains have been identified: personal, family, and social (Borum, 2000; Connor, 2002; Huesmann et al., 2009; Marcus, 2009; Leve & Chamberlain, 2005; Pepler & Craig, 2005; Serbin et al., 2004; U.S. Department of Health and Human Services, Office of the Surgeon General, 2001). Within these three major risk factor domains, fourteen extraneous variables were considered.

The personal risk factor domain that impacts aggression contains six extraneous variables, which were controlled through design (Bordens & Abbott, 2008). According to Leve and Chamberlain (2005), Marcus (2009), Pepler and Craig (2005), and the U.S. Department of Health and Human Services, Office of the Surgeon General (2001), six personal risk factors that are linked to aggression are race, sex, age, academic achievement, depression (an emotional problem), and Attention Deficit Disorder (ADD). Thus, in order to control these six extraneous variables, only African American females who have graduated from high school and who have not been treated for depression or diagnosed with ADD were invited to participate in the study. In addition, only participants who have been classified as young adults (from 21 to 40 years of age) were invited to participate. Hence, through built-in design, the influence of these six personal risk factors on the dependent variable were removed or controlled, thus reducing the possibility of spurious findings (Norusis, 2008).

The family risk factor domain that impacts aggression contains four extraneous variables, which were controlled statistically (Bordens & Abbott, 2008). In other words, the influence of the extraneous variables were statistically removed (Neuman, 2006).

According to Borum (2000), Leve and Chamberlain (2005), Pepler and Craig (2005), and the U.S. Department of Health and Human Services, Office of the Surgeon General (2001), four family risk factors that are linked to aggression are family structure, socioeconomic status, family relations, and siblings. Thus, in order to statistically control these four extraneous variables, the participants were asked to provide information on these variables in the demographics part of the survey. Hence, through statistical analyses, the influence of these four family risk factors on the dependent variable were controlled, thus reducing the possibility of spurious findings (Norusis, 2008).

The social risk factor domain also contains four extraneous variables, which were controlled statistically (Bordens & Abbott, 2008). According to Borum (2000), Pepler and Craig (2005), and the U.S. Department of Health and Human Services, Office of the Surgeon General (2001), four family risk factors that are linked to aggression are school conflict, community conflict, associating with delinquent friends, and residing in a high crime neighborhood. Indeed, each of these variables provides a different social learning experience. In order to statistically control these four extraneous variables, the participants were asked to provide information on these variables in the demographics part of the survey. Hence, through statistical analyses, the influence of these four social risk factors on the dependent variable were controlled, thus reducing the possibility of spurious findings (Norusis, 2008).

In sum, in order to reduce the possibility of spurious findings, relevant extraneous variables need to be considered and controlled (Norusis, 2008). As a result, this study exhibited control over 14 different extraneous variables in the personal, family, and social domains. Indeed, because the extraneous variables in this study covered a wide range of areas that may affect learned aggression, the internal validity of the study was enhanced (Bordens & Abbott, 2008).

Internal Validity

Although the study's design contained several limitations, this particular study did promote internal validity. Internal validity indicates that the research design tests the hypothesis that it is supposed to test (Bordens & Abbott, 2008). In other words, the changes in the dependent variable are due to the changes in the independent variables and not due to some unintended variables (Mertens, 2005). According to Bordens and Abbott, the seven factors that demonstrate internal validity are a) history, b) maturation, c) testing, d) instrumentation, e) statistical regression, f) biased selection of participants, and g) experimental mortality. These factors are discussed below.

The **history factor** involves specific events, other than the treatment, that occur between multiple observations and that may affect the results (Bordens & Abbott, 2008). Because only one observation took place during the study, and because all of the sampling took place within a short amount of time, the history factor was only a minimal threat to the study's internal validity. However, because aggression was measured, controversial social events that may have created anger in society were monitored during the gathering of the data.

The **maturation factor** involves performance change due to age or fatigue (Bordens & Abbott, 2008). For example, a participant may have discontinued answering the questions on the survey before she had finished answering all of the questions. In order to minimize the threat of this factor, the study's survey was short, the questions were easy to answer, and the instruments only required a total of about 20 minutes to complete (Buss & Warren, 2000). Furthermore, the surveys were administered on-line and this allowed the participants to take breaks whenever necessary.

The **testing factor** involves the pretest sensitizing of participants (Bordens & Abbott, 2008). In other words, administering a test prior to treatment may change how the participants respond on a posttest. However, because only a posttest was administered in the study, there was little risk of the testing factor impacting the study's internal validity.

The **instrumentation factor** involves the unobserved changes in researcher criteria or the changes in the sensitivity of the instruments to measure what they are supposed to measure (Bordens & Abbott, 2008). In other words, internal validity is threatened a) if the researcher changes definitions during the data collection process or b) if the measures used to collect data become more or less sensitive over time. Because data in the study were collected via surveys, and because data were collected from each participant only once, the definitions and measures were consistent throughout the study. Indeed, all data from all participants were collected via the same instruments and in the same manner. Furthermore, each participant was given standard instructions. Thus, there was minimal risk of the instrumentation factor impacting the study's internal validity.

The **statistical regression factor** involves recruiting participants for treatment based upon their extreme scores prior to treatment (Bordens & Abbott, 2008). Thus, if measured again, their scores move closer to the population average, regardless of the actual treatment. However, because participants in the study were not selected based on any type of pretest scores, there was little risk of the statistical regression factor impacting the study's internal validity.

The **biased selection of participants factor** involves administering different treatments to different groups and then comparing the groups after the treatment (Bordens & Abbott, 2008). If the groups are not randomly selected, then there is the potential that a group may have pre-existing biases prior to the treatment. Thus, the pre-existing biases and not the treatment may cause differences among the groups. However, because the study's participants were homogeneous (i.e., African American females), and because there was only one group, there was little risk of the biased selection of participants factor impacting the study's internal validity.

The **experimental mortality factor** involves the differential loss of participants from groups, resulting in nonequivalent groups (Bordens & Abbott, 2008). Because the study only considered one group (i.e., African American females) and the participants were surveyed only once, there was little threat of the experimental mortality factor impacting the study's internal validity.

External Validity

In addition to promoting internal validity, the study needs to promote external validity. External validity refers to the extent to which a study's findings can be applied to a target population beyond the specific individuals and settings (Mertens, 2005). According to Bordens and Abbott (2008), the four factors that demonstrate external validity are a) reactive testing, b) interactions between participant selection biases, c) reactive effects of experimental arrangements, and d) multiple treatment interference. These factors are discussed below.

The **reactive testing factor** indicates that a pretest may affect how participants react to the treatment (Bordens & Abbott, 2008). Consequently, the participants' responses may not be representative of the general population. However, because a pretest was not administered in this study, the reactive testing factor posed little threat to the study's external validity.

The **interactions between participant selection biases factor** indicates that by selecting a purposive non-random group, the effects of the treatment may only apply to that group (Bordens & Abbott, 2008). For example, because the study only surveyed African American females, the findings may not be applied to individuals of other races. Thus, in order to minimize the risk of applying the findings to inappropriate groups, the target population's characteristics to which the study's findings may apply have been disclosed.

The **reactive effects of experimental arrangements factor** indicates that because the participants know that they are involved in an experimental treatment, their responses may be artificial (Bordens & Abbott, 2008). However, because the study was non-experimental and participation in contact sports and childhood religion have already occurred, the reactive effects of experimental arrangements posed little threat to the study's external validity. Furthermore, because the surveys were administered on-line and the identities of the participants remained anonymous, there was little motivation for the participants to provide less than truthful responses.

The **multiple treatment interference factor** indicates that, for multiple experimental treatments, the participants' exposure to early treatments may affect the participants' responses to later treatments (Bordens & Abbott, 2008). However, the study was non-experimental and participation in contact sports and childhood religion had already occurred prior to the commencement of the study. Furthermore, data were only collected at one point in time. Thus, the multiple treatment interference factor posed little threat to the study's external validity.

In short, good decisions require valid information. Before we accept any research study's findings as valid, it is imperative that we assess the study's assumptions and limitations. No research study is perfect and the reader must decide if the assumptions and limitations of the study are acceptable. The more we understand research, the more critical we can become in challenging the findings and the less likely we will be deceived.

References

Akers, R.L. (2009). Social learning and social structure: A general theory of crime and deviance. New Brunswick, NJ: Transaction.

Akers, R.L., & Sellers, C.S. (2009). Criminological theories: Introduction, evaluation, and application (5th ed.). New York, NY: Oxford University.

Allison, P.D. (1999). Multiple regression: A primer. Thousand Oaks, CA: Pine Forge.

Antonovich, M.P. (2008). Office and SharePoint 2007 user's guide: Integrating SharePoint with Excel, Outlook, Access, and Word. Berkeley, CA: Apress.

Berg, B.L. (2007). Qualitative research methods for the social sciences (6th ed.). Boston, MA: Pearson.

Berry, B., & Smith, E. (2000). Race, sport, and crime: The misrepresentation of African Americans in team sports and crime. Sociology of Sport Journal, 17(2), 171-197.

Berry, W.D., & Feldman, S. (1985). Multiple regression in practice. Beverly Hills, CA: Sage.

Bordens, K., & Abbott, B. (2008). Research design and methods: A process approach (7th ed.). Boston, MA: McGraw Hill.

Borum, R. (2000). Assessing violence risk among youth. Journal of Clinical Psychology, 56(10), 1263-1288.

Buss, A.H., & Warren, W.L. (2000). Aggression questionnaire manual. Los Angeles, CA: Western Psychological Services.

Champion, D. (2006). Research methods for criminal justice and criminology (3rd ed.). Upper Saddle River, NJ: Pearson Merrill Prentice Hall.

Coakley, J. (2004). Sports in society: Issues & controversies (8th ed.). Boston, MA: McGraw-Hill.

Cohen, J, & Cohen, P. (1983). Applied multiple regression/correlation analysis for the behavioral science (2nd ed.). Hillsdale, NJ: Lawrence Erlbaum.

Connor, D.F. (2002). Aggression and antisocial behavior in children and adolescents: Research and treatment. New York, NY: Guilford.

Creative Research Systems (2010). The survey system: Sample size calculator. Retrieved from http://www.surveysystem.com/sscalc.htm

Davis, W. (2011). A correlational study of childhood religiosity, childhood sport participation, and sport-learned aggression among African American female athletes. (Doctoral dissertation). Retrieved from Dissertation Abstracts International-A. (AAT #3444892)

Durkin, K. (1995). Developmental social psychology: From infancy to old age. Boston, MA: Blackwell.

Field, A. (2005). Discovering statistics using SPSS (2nd ed.). Thousand Oaks, CA: Sage.

Huesmann, L.R., Dubow, E.F., & Boxer, P. (2009). Continuity of aggression from childhood to early adulthood as a predictor of life outcomes: Implications for the adolescent-limited and life-course-persistent models. Aggressive Behavior, 35(2), 136-149. doi:10.1002/ab.20300

Hwang, S., & Akers, R.L. (2003). Substance use by Korean adolescents: A cross-cultural test of the social learning, social bonding, and self-control theories. In R. Akers & G. Jensen (Eds.), Social learning theory and the explanation of crime (p. 39-63). New Brunswick, NJ: Transaction.

Kahane, L.H. (2008). Regression basics (2nd ed.). Los Angeles, CA: Sage.

Leve, L.D., & Chamberlain, P. (2005). Girls in the juvenile justice system: Risk factors and clinical implications. In D. Pepler, K. Madsen, C. Webster, & K. Levene (Eds.), The development and treatment of girlhood aggression (p. 191-215). Mahwah, NJ: Lawrence Erlbaum.

Marcus, R.F. (2009). Cross-sectional study of violence in emerging adulthood. Aggressive Behavior, 35(2), 188-202. doi:10.1002/ab.20293

Mauer, M., & King, R.S. (2007). Uneven justice: State rates of incarceration by race and ethnicity. Retrieved from the Sentencing Project Web site: http://www.sentencing project.org/doc/publications/rd_stateratesofincbyraceandethnicity.pdf

Mertens, D.M. (2005). Research and evaluation in education and psychology: integrating diversity with quantitative, qualitative, and mixed methods (2nd ed.). Thousand Oaks, CA: Sage.

Miracle, A.W., & Rees, C.R. (1994). Lessons from the locker room: The myth of school sports. Amherst, NY: Prometheus.

Neuman, W.L. (2006). Social research methods: Qualitative and quantitative approaches (6th ed.). Boston, MA: Pearson.

Newton, R.P., & Rudestam, K.E. (1999). Your statistical consultant: Answers to your data analysis question. Thousand Oaks, CA: Sage.

Norusis, M.J. (2008). SPSS 16.0 guide to data analysis. Upper saddle River, NJ: Prentice Hall.

Pepler, D.J., & Craig, W.M. (2005). Aggressive girls on troubled trajectories: A developmental perspective. In D. Pepler, K. Madsen, C. Webster, & K. Levene (Eds.), The development and treatment of girlhood aggression (p. 3-28). Mahwah, NJ: Lawrence Erlbaum.

Schroeder, L.D., Sjoquist, D.L., & Stephan, P.E. (1986). Understanding regression analysis: An introductory guide. Newbury Park, CA: Sage.

Serbin, L.A., Stack, D.M., DeGenna, N., Grunzeweig, N., Temcheff, C.E., Schwartzman, A.E., et al. (2004). When aggressive girls become mothers: problems in parenting, health, and development across two generations. In M. Putallaz, & K. Bierman (Eds.), Aggression, antisocial behavior, and violence among girls: A developmental perspective (p. 262-285). New York, NY: Guilford.

Siegel, L. (2003). Criminology (8th ed.). Belmont, CA: Wadsworth-Thomson.

Smith, S., Eggen, M., St. Andre, R. (2006). A transition to advanced mathematics (6th ed.). Belmont, CA: Thomson Brooks/Cole.

Tabachnick, B.G., & Fidell, L.S. (2007). Using multivariate statistics (5th ed.). Boston, MA: Pearson.

U.S. Department of Health and Human Services, Office of the Surgeon General (2001). Youth violence: A report of the Surgeon General. Retrieved from http://www.surgeongeneral.gov/library/youthviolence/default.htm

U.S. Department of Justice, Office of Justice Programs, Office of Juvenile Justice and Delinquency Prevention (1996). Female offenders in the juvenile justice system: Statistics summary. Retrieved from http://www.eric.ed.gov/ERICWebPortal/ search/detailmini.jsp?_nfpb=true&_&ERICExtSearch_SearchValue_0=ED416286& ERICExtSearch_SearchType_0=no&accno=ED416286

U.S. Department of Justice, Office of Justice Programs, Bureau of Justice Statistics (2010). Criminal victimization in the United States, 2007 statistical tables: National crime victimization survey. Retrieved from http://bjs.ojp.usdoj.gov/ c content/pub/pdf/cvus0705.pdf

U.S. Department of Labor, Bureau of Labor Statistics (2010). Annual average unemployment rate, civilian labor force 16 years and over (percent). Retrieved from http://www.bls.gov/cps/prev_yrs.htm

U.S. General Accounting Office (2000). State and federal prisoners: Profiles of inmate characteristics in 1991 and 1997. Retrieved from http://www.gao.gov/archive/ 2000/gg00117.pdf

Walker, S., Spohn, C., & DeLone, M. (2007). The color of justice: race, ethnicity, and crime in America (4th ed.). Belmont, CA: Thomson Wadsworth.

Warner, R.M. (2008). Applied statistics: From bivariate through multivariate techniques. Los Angeles, CA: Sage.

CHAPTER 10. PRACTICAL SCENARIOS

Units Conversions

A unit is a standardized measurement of size (Vorderman, Lewis, Jeffery, & Weeks, 2010).

Example: Convert 20 yards to inches

A * 1 = A   (a value multiplied by 1 does not change)

A / 1 = A   (a value divided by 1 does not change)

(3 ft / 1 yd) has a value of 1

(12 inches / 1 ft) has a value of 1

20 yds = _____ inches

20 yds (1) (1) = 20 yds (3 ft / 1 yd) (12 inches / 1 ft) = 720 inches

This simply changes yard-units to inch-units. The value remains the same.

Problems

1) **Convert 2 tons to ounces;**   2) **Convert 60 MPH to ft/second**

3) **Convert 75,000,000 seconds to years;**   4) **Convert 52 weeks to seconds**

5) **Given: ♥= 77‡   @= 22‡   ♫ = 254♥   121♫ = ☼**

Convert 100 ☼ to @

Fractions, Ratios & Proportions

What is the difference between a fraction and a ratio? A fraction is a set numerical quantity and expresses a number that is part of the whole (the total must be known). A fraction is a way to divide a number into equal parts (Vorderman, et al., 2010). A ratio is a comparison between two or more related quantities. A part-to-part ratio is never a fraction because it does not compare anything to a total amount. However, a part-to-total ratio can be a fraction if it is based on a fixed numeric quantity; a part-to-total ratio is not a fraction if it only represents a relationship pattern. A proportion, which compares the relationship between two sets of quantities, can be determined if a change in one causes a change in the other by a related number.

Example:

A fraction of 1/2 means 1 out of a total of 2, which is 50%. A part-to-part ratio of 1/2 means that for every three items, there will be 1 item A (33%) for every 2 items of B (66%). There is no set numerical quantity. A part-to-total ratio of 1/2 could mean 1 out of a total of 2 (a fraction) or 1 out of every 2 (a relationship pattern).

Solving Equations

Convert 1/2 to fourths (i.e., 1/2 = x/4). If three of the four values are known (e.g., 1, 2, and 4), the unknown number (e.g., X) can be solved by isolating it and making it the subject of the equation (Vorderman et al., 2010). Notice that if the ratios are equal to one another, they will still be equal if all the ratios are inverted. This will become important when the sine rule is considered.

For example: 1/2 = 4/8.   Invert the ratios: 2/1 = 8/4

5/13 = 10/26. Invert the ratios: 13/5 = 26/10

(sin A) / a = (sin B) / b. Invert the ratios: a / (sin A) = b / (sin B)

To convert 1/2 to fourths, set the ratios equal to one another.

1/2 = X/4 . Solve for X.

The equation is a little easier to solve if the unknown value is placed in the numerator. Thus, invert all of the ratios in the equation to ensure that the unknown value is in the numerator. After solving for X, just remember to place it back into the original equation.

Compare the difference in finding X between the two scenarios.

1/2 = x/4 . Solve for x.   4(1/2) = (x/4) 4 => 4/2 = x => x = 2

2/1 = 4/x. Solve for x. x(2/1) = (4/x) x => 2x = 4 => 2x/2 = 4/2 => x = 2

Ratio Problem 1:

Make 18 cubic feet of concrete. Instructions: Mix 2 parts gravel, 3 parts cement, and 4 parts sand. How much of each ingredient is required?

Solution: For every 9 cubic feet on concrete, there will be 2 cubic feet of gravel, 3 cubic feet of cement, and 4 cubic feet of sand.

Therefore,

2/9 cubic feet of gravel = 4/18 cubic feet of gravel

3/9 cubic feet of cement = 6/18 cubic feet of cement

4/9 cubic feet of sand = 8/18 cubic feet of sand

In other words, for every 18 cubic feet of concrete, there will be

4 cubic feet of gravel

6 cubic feet of cement

8 cubic feet of sand

Ratio Problem 2: Using the same ratios in problem 1, if there is 5 cubic feet of gravel and all gravel is to be consumed, how much cement and sand are required?

5 cubic feet of gravel / 2 parts gravel = X / 3 parts cement = Y / 4 parts sand

Thus, for 5 cubic feet of gravel,

X = 7.5 cubic feet cement

Y = 10 cubic feet sand

Make sure that the units are consistent.

Check the Response (use the same ratio)

(2 parts gravel: 3 parts cement: 4 parts sand) = (5 cubic ft gravel: 7.5 cubic ft cements: 10 cubic ft sand)

Same ratio, just magnified by 2.5

Ratio Problem 3:

Problem: A man gets on the elevator in a building and sees that the top floor is floor 20. Each floor is 10 feet tall. He sets up a bungee cord so that after it stretches he will be able to touch the ground with his finger tip. His combined height and reach are 7 feet. Thus, he determines that his stretched bungee cord length will be (20 floors) (10 ft/floor) – 7 feet = 193 feet. He jumps and dies because the bungee cord is 10 feet too long. He failed to consider that the 13th floor did not exist in the building. As an officer, perform a ratio calculation that uses shadows to determine the actual height of the building.   For this exercise, assume that the ground is perfectly flat, that all the shadows are measured within a time period of 15 minutes (to minimize the movement of the sun in the sky), and, because the light source (i.e., the sun) is far from the earth, that the sunlight hits all objects in the same general area on the surface of the earth at the same angle (the rays of light are parallel).

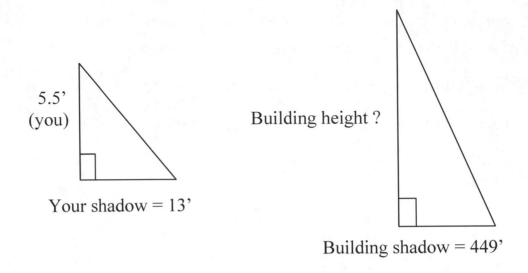

5.5'
(you)

Your shadow = 13'

Building height ?

Building shadow = 449'

Calculate the height of the building by using a building height to building shadow ratio. Show work.

Calculate the height of the building by using your shadow to the building shadow ratio. Show work.

Compare the height of the building to the 193 foot bungee cord.

Vectors & Cartesian Coordinates

A vector is a line that has magnitude and direction. Because velocity has magnitude and direction, it is a vector quantity. Thus, velocity can be represented by a vector on a grid. Speed on the other hand, only has magnitude. Because speed is a scalar quantity, it cannot be represented by a vector on a grid. Cartesian coordinates use an ordered pair of numbers to identify a point on a grid. On a grid, the horizontal coordinate (East, West) is listed first and the vertical coordinate (North, South) is listed second (Vorderman et al., 2010). East and North are positive (right and up) while West and South are negative (left and down). The top of the map is always North. For example, (4, 2) means to move 4 units to the East (right) and 2 units to the North (up). Because West is negative East and South is negative North, (-3, -1) means to move 3 units West (left) and 1 unit South (down).

The kickoff returner in football is told to run north and not to run east or west. This means to run the ball toward the opposing team's goal line. If a kickoff returner runs from sideline to sideline, the opposing team will tackle the returner with minimal yardage gained. This idea applies to adding vectors and for determining coordinates. Distinguish between North/South and East/West. North/South is one plane; East/West is another plane. When summing vectors that utilize directions in both planes, the vectors must be broken down and the components in one plane must be assessed separately from the components in the other plane. For example, add up all of the East and West directions for a final position in the East/West plane. Then add up all of the North and South directions for a final position in the North/South plane. Do not add East and West directions to the North and South plane and do not add North and South directions to the East and West plane.

As stated earlier, when coordinates are placed inside the parentheses, they will have the following format: (E, N). South is a negative North. West is a negative East.

1) Start at 3W, 2 N. What are the final coordinates after the following movements are made?

11N + 2E + 1S + 2W = _____

2) You are at 3W, 5S. Your partner is at 5E, 7N. What is the shortest distance between you two?

3) Start from (0,0). Plot the following items of evidence on a chart.

Chair = (-4, 5)

Gun = (7, 6)

Hat = (-1, -4)

Coat = (10, -3)

4) Calculate the distance between the following items as plotted in problem 3.

1) Chair, Gun

2) Chair, Hat

3) Chair, Coat

4) Gun, Hat

5) Gun, Coat

6) Hat, Coat

Crash Analysis

Velocity = speed with direction;   Speed = distance / time;   **S = d / t**

Example: distance / time = 50 MPH = 50 miles / 1 hour

Exercise 1

If a vehicle travels 75 miles in 45 minutes, what is the average speed in MPH?

First, convert 45 minutes to hours

(45 minutes) · (1 hour / 60 minutes) = 0.75 hours

Speed = 75 miles / 0.75 hours = 100 MPH

Exercise 2

If a vehicle travels 100 miles at 40 MPH and on the return trip travels 100 miles at 60 MPH, what is the vehicle's average speed in MPH for the entire trip of 200 miles?

Incorrect: Average Speed = (40 MPH + 60 MPH) / 2 = 50 MPH

Correct: Average Speed = total distance / total time = (100 miles + 100 miles) / total time

Need to calculate total time

Speed = distance / time;   time = distance / speed

$Time_1$ = 100 miles / 40 miles/hour = 2.5 hours

$Time_2$ = 100 miles / 60 miles/hour = 1.67 hours

Total Time = $Time_1$ + $Time_2$ = 2.5 hours + 1.67 hours = 4.17 hours

It is important to note that the vehicle traveled at 60 MPH for less time than at 40 MPH.

Thus, Average Speed = 200 miles / 4.17 hours = 48 MPH

Exercise 3: Scenario

At 2:00 am, there was a report of a shooting on I-80 MP 122 EB. You are off of the highway, but can safely get to the highway in 5 minutes. You will enter the highway at MP 134, which is 12 miles east of the shooting. There is a service area at MP 125 EB, which has a gas station and restaurant. There is an exit at MP 144 EB, which is 2 miles south of the Michigan border. There is also a toll booth at MP 156 EB, which is 2 miles west of the Ohio border. The typical speed for tractor-trailers is 70 MPH. The top speed for your police vehicle is 140 MPH. The suspect vehicle is described as a blue/white **cab-over** tractor-trailer with the name "Falcon" on it.

Q1: Once you get to I-80 MP 134, about where will the suspect vehicle be in relation to you?

About 2 minutes after you get to the highway, you notice a blue/white **conventional** tractor-trailer with the word "Falcon" on it. At the same time, another police officer radios to you that the suspect vehicle may have pulled into the service area at MP 125 EB. The other officer states that he will be at the service area in 4 minutes.

Q2: Do you head east and try to stop the conventional (not cab-over) tractor-trailer that passed you or do you head west and rendezvous with the other officer?

Q3: What type of stop is this, and how should the stop be carried out?

Q4: If the blue/white tractor-trailer that passed you was the suspect vehicle, how long do you have before it will be too late to stop the vehicle?

Q5: If you decide to head east to stop the blue/white suspect vehicle, at what mile marker will you stop the vehicle if the vehicle has a 5 mile head start and if you expect the vehicle to travel at 70 MPH so as not to draw attention?

Q6: Suppose the shooting was reported to the police department 5 minutes after the shooting took place and the tractor-trailer traveled at 77 MPH once it left the crime scene. How many miles will the tractor-trailer have traveled and will you see the vehicle pass you at MP 134 EB if you arrive there 5 minutes after the shooting is reported to you?

Crash Scene Measurement Determinations

See *Table 19* for important formulas needed to solve problems in the field. Some of the formulas only apply to right triangles. Other formulas may be applied to triangles that are not right angled.

Table 19

Triangle Rules and Formulas (Large, 2006)

Pythagorean theorem	$(hypotenuse)^2 =$ $(opposite\ leg)^2 + (adjacent\ leg)^2$	Right triangle $c^2 = a^2 + b^2$	
Sine ratio	$\sin \phi$ = opposite leg / hypotenuse	Right triangle	
Cosine ratio	$\cos \phi$ = adjacent leg / hypotenuse	Right triangle	
Tangent ratio	$\text{Tan } \phi$ = opposite leg / adjacent leg	Right triangle	
Sine rule	a / sin A = b / sin B = c / sin C	Right + Non-right-angled triangles	
Sine rule	sin A / a = sin B / b = sin C / c	Right + Non-right-angled triangles	

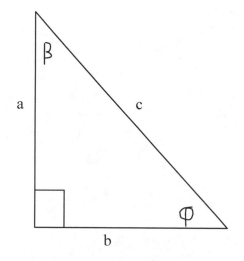

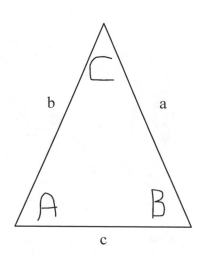

175

Calculating the Angle of Impact of Blood Splatter (Saferstein, 2011)

Equation: sin (A) = width of bloodstain / length of bloodstain,

where A = the angle of impact ± 5° error

Stain Number	Width of Bloodstain	Length of Bloodstain	Sine A	Estimated Impact Angle
_____	_____	_____	___	_____
_____	_____	_____	___	_____
_____	_____	_____	___	_____
_____	_____	_____	___	_____
_____	_____	_____	___	_____

Consider each bloodstain independently. Below are bloodstains discovered on the floor. At what angle did each bloodstain hit the surface? Take measurements.

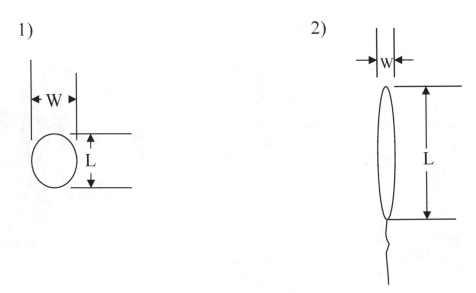

1)

2)

3)   4)   5)

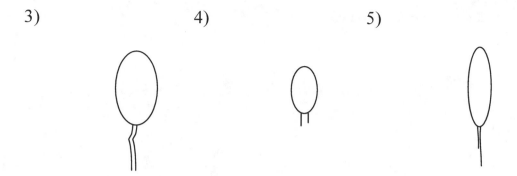

Consider each bloodstain independently. Assume that the bloodstains on the floor are from a victim who is 6 feet tall and who has a gunshot wound that is 5 feet from the ground when the victim is standing upright. For each of the above bloodstains, how far was the victim standing from the bloodstain on the floor? In other words, find X (see below).

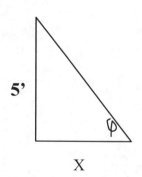

1) _____   2) _____   3) _____   4) _____   5) _____

Determine distances for a crash report.

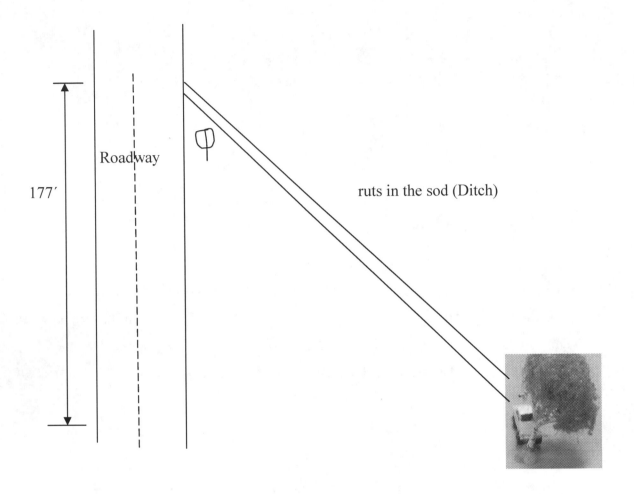

Roadway

177′

ruts in the sod (Ditch)

Q1: If ϕ = 23 degrees, what is the distance of the ruts in the sod?

Q2: How far is the car from the roadway?

Determine distance and angle for a crash report.

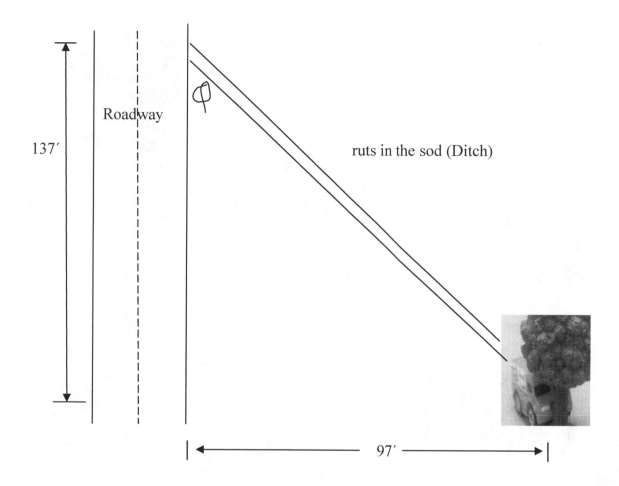

Q1: What is the distance of the ruts in the sod?

Q2: What is the angle φ in degrees that the vehicle veered off of the roadway?

Determine distances and angles for a Fire Scene.

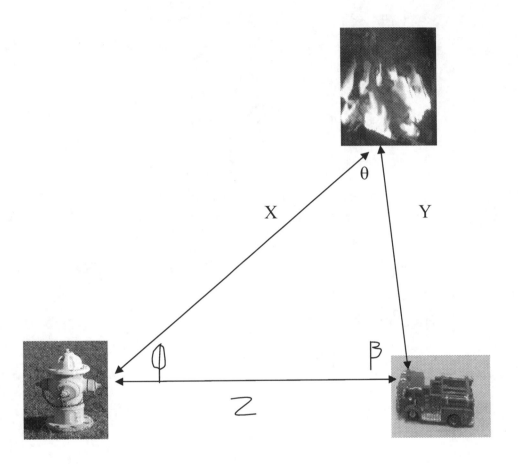

Q1: If X = 233′, Y = 68′, β = 44°, find Z.

Q2: If X = 423′, β = 53°, ⏀ = 72°, find Y.

Q3: If Z = 89′, Y = 22′, θ = 54°, find β.

Q4: If Z = 113′, X = 193′, β = 51°, find θ.

RADAR

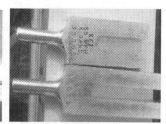

Figure 7. Police Radar.

To accurately measure a vehicle's true speed using radar, the radar must measure the vehicle's speed head-on (i.e., 0 degrees off set). The police radar sends out radar waves that bounce off of the approaching vehicle (Doppler Effect). Decreasing the time between successive radar waves will produce an increasing speed on the radar. If the vehicle approaches the radar head-on, the time between radar waves will decrease at a greater rate than if the vehicle approaches the radar at an angle. In other words, the shortest distance and quickest time between two points is a straight line. If the police radar is off at an angle, the measured speed will not be complete and true; the radar will only measure a component of the actual speed. The difference between the actual speed and the measured speed is due to cosine error.

The formula for determining the vehicle's speed is

Speed indicated on Radar = Vrs = V_1 (cos β)

Vrs = Vehicle speed as indicated on police radar

V_1 = Vehicle's actual speed

β = the angle between the vehicle's actual direction and the direction toward the Radar

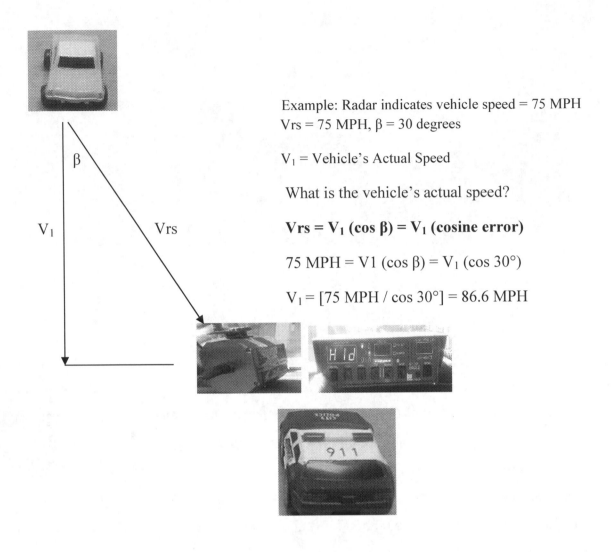

Example: Radar indicates vehicle speed = 75 MPH

Vrs = 75 MPH, β = 30 degrees

V_1 = Vehicle's Actual Speed

What is the vehicle's actual speed?

Vrs = V_1 (cos β) = V_1 (cosine error)

75 MPH = V1 (cos β) = V_1 (cos 30°)

V_1 = [75 MPH / cos 30°] = 86.6 MPH

What happens to the Radar speed when the vehicle passes the police car (β = 90°)?

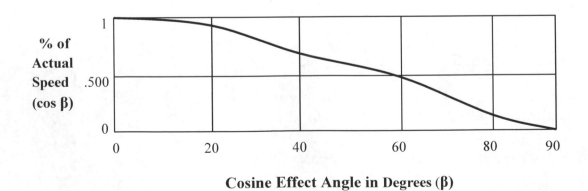

Cosine Effect Angle in Degrees (β)

Figure 8. Cosine Error (Sawicki, 2013).

182

Police radar clock and driver's argument in court.

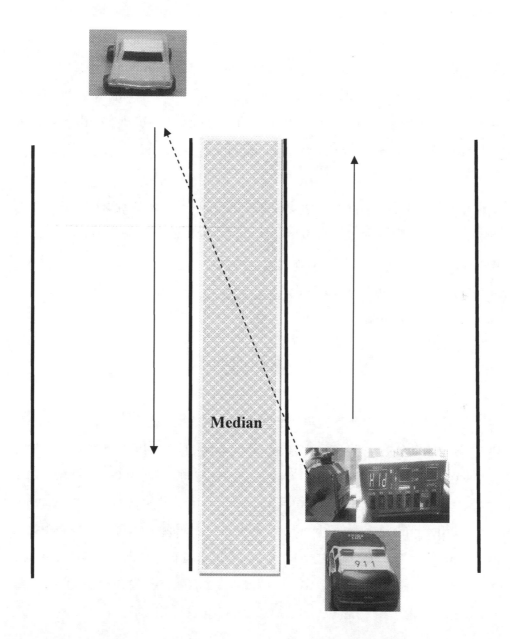

The police officer argued in court that he used an accurate radar gun on the highway and clocked an approaching car at 77 MPH, which passed the police vehicle in the opposite direction. The driver argued in court that he was not traveling at 77 MPH and that the radar was wrong because the radar was at a 20 degree angle relative to the car's direction of travel. Does the driver of the car have a valid argument based on the angle? Did the radar gun ever indicate that the speed of the approaching car was actually zero MPH?

It is very important for police officers to develop a tracking history to confirm that they have clocked the correct vehicle. Although the radar device displays a number that represents the oncoming vehicle's speed, the radar does not tell the officer which vehicle was speeding. One state police department, for example, requires officers to qualify with the radar before they are allowed to use the radar for traffic enforcement. The qualification includes having the officers accurately estimate the speeds of vehicles within plus or minus 5 miles per hour. The radar is then used to confirm the estimated speeds.

The radar beam relies on three factors to determine vehicle speed: reflectivity (the biggest beam reflected back to the radar), position (the closest vehicle to the radar), and speed (the fastest vehicle) (P.B. Electronics Inc., n.d.). Radars are equipped with a speaker that provides a tone that can be used to track a vehicle. The tone's pitch will change as the vehicle passes the police radar.

VASCAR

Unlike radar, which clocks instantaneous speed, the VASCAR (Visual Average Speed Computer And Recorder) device is used to calculate a vehicle's average speed. The VASCAR has the capability to record time and distance in order to calculate a vehicle's average speed. The police officer will measure the amount of time that a car travels from one point to another and, as part of the clock, will also measure the distance between the two points. Example: Using a VASCAR, assume the distance that a car traveled was 0.25 miles and the time it took the vehicle to cover that distance was 12.6 seconds. The average speed = distance / time = [0.25 miles / 12.6 seconds] = 71.4 MPH.

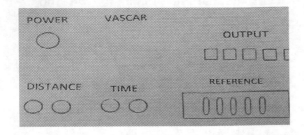

Figure 9. Sketch of Police VASCAR.

Collision Analysis

Skidmarks may be used to determine the pre-crash speeds of vehicles at crash scenes (Faulkner, 2009; Schultz & Hunt, 1999). This may be very important during crash investigations. One of the duties that a police officer may have is to determine the cause of each crash. Thus, understanding how skidmarks are related to a vehicle's speed prior to its impact is necessary for an effective police crash investigation. One technique used to determine a vehicle's pre-crash speed is to use the driver's stated speed and to collect skidmarks, which will be used to determine the friction coefficient factor. Once this value is obtained, it will be used with the actual skidmarks to determine the vehicle's pre-crash speed. See below for an example.

Variables

V = velocity of vehicle in MPH

S = skid distance in feet

f = % coefficient of friction

Equation

$$V^2 = 30 \, (S)(f); \quad \text{Therefore, } V = [30 \, (S) \, (f) \,]^{1/2}$$

Example

The driver stated that he was traveling at **35 MPH** and the actual skid mark at the scene is **100 feet**. To determine a **quick rough estimate** of the **minimum** vehicle speed prior to the collision, **assume a roadway friction coefficient of 60%,** which is in the general area of many road surfaces (Schultz & Hunt, 1999).

Therefore,

$$V^2 = 30 \, S \, f = 30 \, (100 \text{ feet}) \, (.60) = 1800$$

$$V = (1800)^{1/2} = 42.4 \text{ MPH}$$

However, upon investigation, the vehicle has sustained much damage. Hence, the car was probably traveling much faster than 42.4 MPH prior to impact because the vehicle still had momentum at impact. If further investigation is deemed necessary, a more accurate minimum speed (prior to the collision) can be calculated. Although the weight of the vehicle and the condition of the tires and brakes do not significantly impact speed calculations, the jury may perceive otherwise (Schultz & Hunt, 1999). Therefore, whenever possible, the actual car that was involved in the crash should be used to determine speed calculations. All variables surrounding the crash investigation should be aligned to match the conditions of the vehicle prior to the crash, which include location of the crash and the direction of travel. Because crash speed investigations can be dangerous, great care should be exercised when obtaining skid marks. Legal speeds should be employed.

To test the accuracy of the driver's statement of vehicle speed prior to the collision, the crash investigator will perform some tests. However, the coefficient of friction must be established prior to the calculations. There are several ways to determine the coefficient of friction at the crash scene: 1) assess it by collecting skid marks and then use an established chart to read the value; 2) assess it by using a Pavement Drag Factor Table for Rubber Tires; or 3) assess it by using a coefficient of friction measuring device at the scene (drag sled).

First, charts may be available that correlate vehicle speed, the coefficient of friction, and skid mark distance (Schultz & Hunt, 1999). If two of the variables are known, the third can be determined by reading the chart. However, if the actual speed that is needed to measure the skid marks at the scene is too great, then the coefficient of friction should be measured via a coefficient of friction measuring tool. See *Figure 10* Skidmark Chart.

Suppose a driver was involved in a crash and he states that he was traveling at 35 MPH. Furthermore, there is much damage to the vehicle due to a head on collision with a concrete barrier on the shoulder of the road. Suppose the officer has no drag sled and no chart for the possible ranges for pavement drag factors for rubber tires. However, suppose the officer does have the *Figure 10* skidmark chart. The officer can determine the vehicle's

186

pre-crash speed, but the officer must first determine the coefficient of friction. This can be accomplished by actually performing a skidmark test at the crash scene.

To determine the coefficient of friction, the investigator will drive his vehicle at a predetermined test speed. For example, let the test speed be 25 MPH. The officer will collect his own information for three skid marks. The longest skid mark will be used because this will translate to a lower coefficient of friction at a given speed (this gives the driver the benefit of the doubt by accepting a longer skidmark for a fixed speed). Once the longest of three skid marks has been determined, the coefficient of friction will be obtained by reading the chart.

Suppose the crash investigator traveled at **25 MPH** and measured three skid marks: **44 feet, 48 feet, and 50 feet.** Using *Figure 10*, the speed of 25 MPH and skid mark of 50 feet intersect at the **55% friction coefficient factor**. Now, the 55% friction coefficient factor can be intersected with the 100' skid mark to determine the vehicles pre-crash speed, which is about 42 MPH, according to *Figure 10*. This 55% friction coefficient value will also be placed back into the speed formula.

Using the formula to determine speed, below is the estimate of pre-crash vehicle speed based on friction coefficient factor and **actual** skid marks.

$$V = (30 \text{ S f})^{1/2} = [30 \ (100') \ (.55)]^{1/2} \quad \therefore \quad V = 40.6 \text{ MPH}$$

Compare this value to the **quick estimate speed**, which was 42.4 MPH, and to the speed as determined by the skidmark chart, which was about 42 MPH.

However, it should be noted that the actual skid mark was cut short due to the collision. This means that the vehicle was able to slow down about 40 MPH prior to impact, which means that the vehicle was traveling much faster than 40 MPH prior to impact (notice that the 40.6 MPH is the pre-crash speed). This contradicts the driver's statement that he was only traveling at 35 MPH (which includes the speed slowed down + the speed at impact). An expert will have to be called in to determine the speed of the vehicle at the time of impact based on the amount of damage to the vehicle. The vehicle's true speed prior to collision will be determined by summing the speed that the vehicle decelerated and the amount of speed at impact.

TOTAL SPEED = speed slowed down + speed at impact

In sum, an officer will collect three test skidmarks at a fixed speed to assess the friction coefficient factor. Once this value is obtained, it will be used with the actual crash scene skidmarks to determine the vehicle's pre-crash speed.

Skidmark Chart

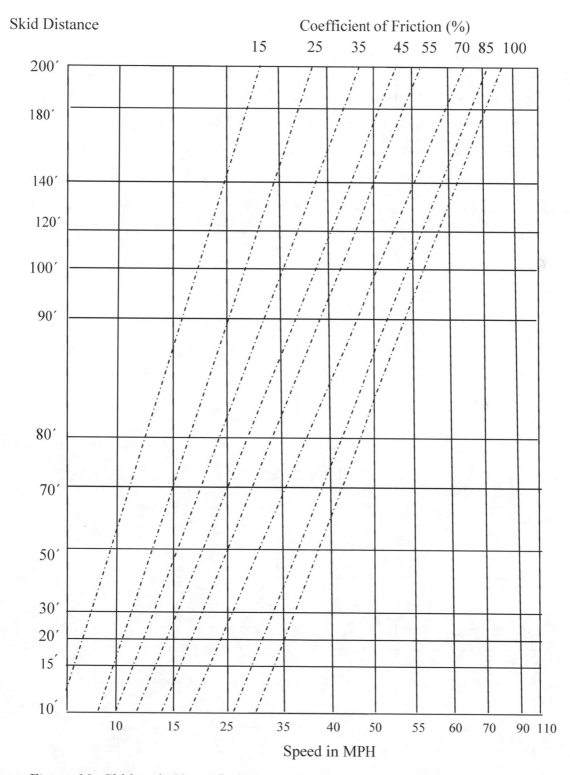

Figure 10. Skidmark Chart (fictitious).

Ranges of Pavement Drag Factors for Rubber Tires

Second, charts may be available that describe the possible ranges for pavement drag factors for rubber tires (Faulkner, 2009; Schultz & Hunt, 1999). These charts will describe the road surface, weather conditions, and speed differentials. Thus, the investigator will simply find the conditions that match the pre-crash conditions at the crash scene and the investigator will take the average of the coefficient of friction values on the chart. For example, for a new dry asphalt road surface less than 25 MPH, the coefficient of friction range is .77 to .88, so the average value of .825 will be used. See *Table 20* for an example of a fictitious chart for pavement drag factors for rubber tires.

Table 20

Chart for Pavement Drag Factors for Rubber Tires (Fictitious)

Ranges of Pavement Drag Factors for Rubber Tires (coefficient of friction - fictitious values)								
Road Surface Description	Dry				Wet			
	≤ 25 MPH		> 25 MPH		≤ 25 MPH		> 25 MPH	
	From	To	From	To	From	To	From	To
Asphalt								
New	.77	.88	.69	.77	.57	.68	.49	.57
Traveled	.71	.85	.68	.76	.51	.65	.48	.56
Excessive Tar	.67	.77	.63	.68	.57	.57	.43	.48
Concrete								
New	.75	.86	.71	.80	.55	.66	.51	.60
Grooved	.79	.85	.72	.79	.59	.65	.52	.59
Traveled	.69	.79	.67	.75	.49	.59	.47	.55

With Shells	.66	.77	.64	.74	.46	.57	.44	.54

Brick							
New	.71	.79	.69	.76	.51	.59	.49	.56
Traveled	.64	.70	.61	.74	.44	.50	.41	.54

Gravel							
Packed	.55	.59	.52	.58	.35	.39	.32	.38
Loose	.49	.56	.44	.50	.29	.36	.24	.30

Dirt							
Packed	.55	.61	.50	.57	.35	.41	.30	.37
Oil covered	.52	.55	.49	.55	.32	.35	.29	.35
Loose	.44	.49	.41	.48	.24	.29	.21	.28

Chip-seal							
Packed	.72	.81	.69	.77	.52	.81	.49	.57
Loose	.49	.59	.45	.50	.29	.59	.25	.30

Cobblestone							
New	.70	.77	.65	.72	.50	.77	.45	.52
Worn	.67	.76	.63	.69	.47	.76	.43	.49

Snow							
Packed	.22	.29	.11	.19	.05	.29	.03	.02
Loose	.11	.16	.04	.11	.04	.16	.02	.01

Metal							
Ridged	.72	.77	.67	.72	.52	.77	.47	.52
Smooth	.61	.69	.55	.62	.41	.69	.35	.42

Glass								
Grooved	.78	.86	.70	.76	.38	.56	.20	.30
Smooth	.71	.85	.65	.73	.31	.55	.25	.28

Example:

What was the vehicle's pre-crash speed if the road surface was new wet cobblestone, the driver stated that he was traveling at 40 MPH, and the vehicle left a 231 foot skidmark?

New wet cobblestone greater than 25 MPH: coefficient of friction = .45 to .52

Actual Skidmarks = 231′

The average coefficient of friction value is .485

$$V^2 = 30 \, (S)(f); \quad \text{Therefore, } V = [30 \, (S) \, (f) \,]^{1/2}$$

$$V = [30 \, (231′) \, (.485)]^{1/2} \quad \therefore \quad V = 57.9 \text{ MPH}$$

Drag Sled

A drag sled can be used to calculate the coefficient of friction for a road surface, but the units in the calculation for the coefficient of friction must equal one (i.e., cancel out). The goal is to divide Newtons by Newtons so that there are no units left for the coefficient of friction. In other words, the units for weight need to be in the form of Newtons (e.g., if you measured weight in pounds, you will need to convert it to Newtons because force is measured in Newtons). The equation for the frictional force is below.

Frictional force = frictional coefficient * normal force

Normal force is the perpendicular component of contact force exerted on an object by the surface. The object also exerts a force on the surface. When there is no angle, these forces are opposite and equal. By rearranging the equation above, we get the equation for the coefficient of friction.

f = coefficient of friction = Frictional Force/Weight

The investigator can measure the coefficient of friction directly at the scene by using a coefficient of friction measuring tool, such as a drag sled (Faulkner, 2009). See *Figure 11*. This provides the advantage of collecting first-hand information. However, not all officers have drag sleds. When a drag sled is used, the force needed to move the drag sled must remain consistent for an accurate F value reading.

Drag factor equation: f = **F / W**

where,

f = coefficient of friction,   F = force needed to move sled (N),   W= weight of sled (N)

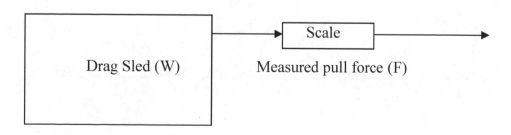

Figure 11. Drag Sled.

Example: Find the coefficient of friction for the road surface.

Given:

Drag sled weighs 40 lbs = W

F = Pull force = 60 N of force

Solution: Note: 1 lb = 4.4482216 N

Coefficient of friction = f = F / W = 60 N / 40 lbs (4.4482216 N / lb) = .337

Problems (use the information in this chapter to answer the questions)

1) What is the range of coefficient of friction?

Brick, new, dry, > 25 MPH = _____

Snow, packed, wet, < 25 MPH = _____

2) Determine the coefficient of friction for 3 different surfaces (best estimate).

    1)   Test speed = 60 MPH; Skid test = 28', 33', 40'   f = _____

    2)   Test speed = 43 MPH; Skid test = 72', 76', 80'   f = _____

    3)   Test speed = 80 MPH; Skid test = 92', 98', 101'   f = _____

3) Crash Scene: Determine the minimum speed during 3 different crashes.

S = skid distance in feet

f = coefficient of friction

S = 70'; f = .33   speed _____

S = 100'; f = .56   speed _____

S = 144"; f = .80   speed _____

4) Drag Sled

Drag sled weighs = 50 lbs;   Pull force = 22 N;   Coefficient of friction = _____

Drag sled weighs = 37 lbs;   Pull force = 30 N;   Coefficient of friction = _____

Drag sled weighs = 51 lbs;   Pull force = 160 N;   Coefficient of friction = _____

Drag sled weighs = 44 lbs;   Pull force = 90 N;   Coefficient of friction = _____

References

Faulkner, D. (2009). *Collision investigation for the patrol officer* (2nd ed.). San Clemente, CA: Law Tech.

Large, L. (2006). *Illustrated dictionary of math.* Saffron Hill, London: Usborne.

P.B. Electronics Inc. (n.d.). *Police radar.* Retrieved from http://www.pbelectronics.com/police_radar.htm

Saferstein, R. (2011). *Criminalistics: An introduction to forensic science* (10th ed.). Upper Saddle River, NJ: Prentice.

Sawicki, D. (2013). *Cosine effect error: Microwave and laser radar.* Retrieved from http://www.copradar.com/preview/chapt2/ch2d1.html

Schultz, D. O., & Hunt, D.D. (1999). *Traffic: Investigation and enforcement* (3rd ed.). Belmont, CA: Wadsworth.

Vorderman, C., Lewis, B., Jeffery, A., & Weeks, M. (2010). *Help your kids with math.* New York: NY: Dorling Kindersley.